Fly Fishing the Seasons in
COLORADO

Help Us Keep This Guide Up to Date

Every effort has been made by the author and editors to make this guide as accurate and useful as possible. However, many things can change after a guide is published—fish populations fluctuate, rules and regulations change, techniques evolve, sites and other facilities come under new management, Mother Nature asserts her will, and so on.

We would appreciate hearing from you concerning your experiences with this guide and how you feel it could be improved and kept up to date. While we may not be able to respond to all comments and suggestions, we'll take them to heart, and we'll also make certain to share them with the author. Please send your comments and suggestions to the following address:

GPP
Reader Response/Editorial Department
P.O. Box 480
Guilford, CT 06437

Or you may e-mail us at:

editorial@globepequot.com

Thanks for your input, and happy angling!

Fly Fishing the Seasons in
COLORADO

An Essential Guide for Fishing through the
Winter, Spring, Summer, and Fall

Ron Baird

LYONS PRESS
Guilford, Connecticut
An imprint of Globe Pequot Press

To my grandchildren: Payton, Logan, and Brody Jones.
May you always have healthy trout waters to fish.

To buy books in quantity for corporate use
or incentives, call **(800) 962–0973**
or e-mail **premiums@GlobePequot.com.**

Lyons Press is an imprint of Globe Pequot Press.

Text design: Sheryl P. Kober
Project editor: Julie Marsh
Layout: Sue Murray
Maps by Daniel Lloyd © Morris Book Publishing LLC

Library of Congress Cataloging-in-Publication Data
Baird, Ron.
  Fly fishing the seasons in Colorado : an essential guide for fishing through the winter, spring,
summer, and fall / Ron Baird.
       p. cm.
  Includes index.
  ISBN 978-0-7627-7170-7
  1. Fly fishing—Colorado. 2. Seasons—Colorado. I. Title.
  SH475.B344 2012
  688.7'912409788—dc23
                                                                                    2011033868

Printed in the United States of America
10 9 8 7 6 5 4 3 2 1

CONTENTS

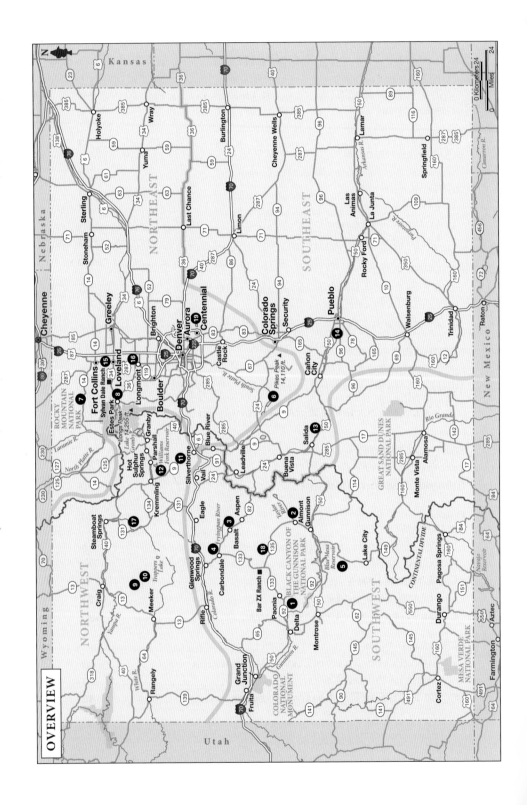

OVERVIEW

ACKNOWLEDGMENTS

I would like to express my sincere gratitude to the following people and organizations who made this book possible and very much *better.*

Joe Novosad, a friend and Globe Pequot distributor—who suggested me for the opportunity, for this one as well as for my first book, *Fishing Colorado: An Angler's Complete Guide to More than 125 Top Fishing Spots.*

Allen Jones—My fierce acquisitions editor who conceived the concept of this book and who tried his best to keep me on track.

Julie Marsh—Globe Pequot project editor who caught the errors and inconsistencies in the manuscript and made the book eminently more readable.

Front Range Anglers—whose staff was with me all the way, particularly Russell Miller and Jon Spiegel, who supplied so much of the fine photography for the book.

Bill Edrington of Royal Gorge Anglers—who has solved so many of the riddles of fishing the Arkansas River and shared them with me.

Kirk Webb of Taylor Creek Fly Shop—who was never too busy to answer my questions and provide expert advice and photographs of the Fryingpan and Roaring Fork Rivers.

Cutthroat Anglers—whose website provided much information about fishing the enigmatic Blue River and Williams Fork tailwater.

Rod Cesario of Dragonfly Anglers—for expert advice on the Taylor River.

RIGS Flyshop—which helped me get in touch with professional photographer Jack Brauer, who supplied the wonderful photograph of the Gunnison Gorge that leads off the book.

Jack Brauer—world-class nature photographer for his graciousness and his photograph of the Gunnison Gorge.

Ben Olson of Black Canyon Anglers—who early on helped me update the condition of the Gunnison Gorge in the wake of a flash flood in 2010, and for other timely information.

Tim Romano—whose excellent photographs fleshed out the book.

Kendall Bakich of the Colorado Division of Wildlife—for updated fish population in the Fryingpan River.

Oscar Marks of the Gunnison River Anglers—who filled in the knowledge holes on the mysterious Lake Fork of the Gunnison River.

Jay Zimmerman of Rocky Mountain Anglers—for advice and great fly designs.

Dean Billington of Bull Basin Outfitters—for photographs and excellent advice.

To my wife Nancy—who put up with it all.

All the advice I received was accurate. Any mistakes are my own.

INTRODUCTION

The purpose of this book is to give anglers—beginner or intermediate, new to the state, or old-timers—the opportunity to maximize their chances for success. While there's nothing I can do to improve your casting skills, almost every other facet of trout fishing is based upon making good decisions, a process that needs—first and foremost—access to good, up-to-date information.

Of all the variables that affect a smart angler's technique on a given stretch of water, perhaps the greatest is simply the season in which the angler has chosen to fish. Changing weather impacts habitat and hatches, which impact feeding habits, which in turn change how we need to approach the water. A fishery that you've come to know very well in the spring or summer will become, with cold weather and lower water flows, almost unrecognizable in the fall and winter. Knowing what to expect from a given location in a given season, and then changing your plans accordingly, is absolutely key to a fisherman's success.

In this book, within each season each fishery is divided into sections that include a description of the location; narrative snippets regarding history or stories of the area; comments on the health of the fishery; information on stream flows (very important!); advice on access, strategies, and tactics; and Pro Tips.

In addition to information relating to seasonal variability, the appendices include more general information on wading safety; Internet resources for determining stream flows and more specific information on hatches and local conditions; phone numbers and addresses for local fly shops and outfitting/guiding services; and information on New Zealand mud snail and zebra and quagga mussel control.

SUMMER

Colorado's summer fishing season in many rivers and streams begins as the runoff clears and drops and ends as the water begins to cool in September. This is particularly true in middle and lower altitude waters that have no major impoundments upstream, otherwise known as freestone waters. Primary examples of these are the Cache La Poudre River, the middle and lower Colorado River, and the Arkansas River. Each of these is a fine fishery. In recent years the runoff period has ranged from 3 weeks to 2 months, depending upon snowpack and weather.

Other rivers, such as the legendary South Platte, are heavily dammed, so they stay lower later in the spring season. When irrigation waters are unleashed later in the spring and summer, water levels can rise dramatically and quickly. Stretches of these impounded rivers are world-class fisheries, while lesser known stretches of the South Platte River, such as Eleven Mile Canyon, are also very good.

In high altitude areas, those generally above 9,000 feet, the summer season begins in late June, at ice-out, and lasts until ice-over in October or November.

The state of Colorado's surface-water website, which contains real-time and historic river and stream flow rates (see Appendix C), is an invaluable tool for helping a fisherman predict when a given area might become fishable.

If you notice stream flow information that indicates summerlike conditions (high but decreasing stream flows and, hopefully, clear water), it might mean that stoneflies are going off. These can be fished as nymphs in the mornings, as the bugs tend to hatch at night this time of the year. The bigger, dry flies can be brought out later in the day.

There might also still be some blue-winged olive (BWO) mayflies, fishable with both nymphs and dry flies. And pale morning dun (PMD) mayfly nymphs will be maturing and floating free. In some rivers green drake mayflies will start hatching as the water level comes down, as will caddisflies, although the time varies quite a bit in different waters. Put together, these

Colorado's summer opens up a number of high country lakes, giving fishermen access to trout that have had a whole winter in which to build up an appetite.
TIM ROMANO

various hatches provide a veritable feast for the hungry fish and a free-for-all for anglers.

Weighted nymphs and emergers of all species should be fished along the bank and through any smooth spots in the fast water and in backwaters that curl along the banks. Even though the water is still fast, a big, bushy attractor such as a green, orange, or yellow Stimulator can produce a quick hit, because the fish don't have much time to scope a bug out.

In some spots during the early summer, fish will feed throughout the day, secure in the cool, fast water. As the flow gets lower, more and more slow spots will open up to dry flies. With the multitude of flies still on the water, an angler should find a spot that looks good and cast a given fly only a few times. If it doesn't receive a look, consider changing to another fly type, either in nymphs, emergers, or dry flies.

Approximate sizes for flies can be estimated by turning over rocks to see the nymphal forms or by watching bugs that are flying over water. The only time an angler needs to be exact is in the tailwaters below dams. Most of the time close is good enough. Fish will still key on a single species or more likely a stage of a species, but it's often hard to tell from watching. Only blanket hatches, such as the world-famous Tax Day Brachycentrus caddis on the Arkansas, demand that a single species of fly be used. And these hatches are so prolific they bring their own difficulties: It's sometime hard to get the fish to notice your fly because there are also thousands of real bugs on the water.

On tailwater fisheries the midge hatch never really stops, so many anglers will often trail a midge nymph beneath a dry fly or an emerger with great success.

By late July the water will usually have dropped and become warmer, and the best action shifts to mornings and evenings. Caddis, particularly, will only hatch in the shade or when the sun drops beyond the horizon. Hoppers splashed noisily will bring a fish to the surface, and both beetles and hoppers will move fish during the day.

When the water reaches its warmest temperature of the day (3 to 4 p.m.) the fish, particularly rainbows, will move into the riffles to get more oxygen and, yes, to eat. Big, bushy, high-floating dry flies, usually attractors, can be cast over and over again in the riffle water. It may take a number of passes before the fish will bite. Once, on the Lake Fork of the Gunnison, I had a strong feeling that a big fish was sitting in a smooth area between two barely submerged rocks about 3 feet apart, and I cast to it at least 30 times with no action. On the next cast I hooked and landed an 18-inch brown. It was the only bite I had had in 3 days. Though it happened in the evening, the same thing works during the day, more for rainbows than browns, but I normally wouldn't cast more than 10 to 15 times over the same small area and would then move to another spot. Don't be afraid to try that with large nymphs such as a #12 Hare's Ear or Pheasant Tail, either bead head or lightly weighted.

High altitude lakes follow the same pattern, temperature wise, as running water. Fish are active early in the season when the water is cooler, later in the summer when it's cloudy, or in the mornings and evenings. If fish are rising, cast a dry fly imitating whatever bugs are present as close as possible to a rise ring. If the fish aren't rising, try a lightly weighted emerger, retrieved with a wrist roll, and slowly stripped in 3- to 4-inch jerks. Let it settle for 5 to 10 seconds between retrieves.

The two major hatches on most high altitude still waters are damselflies (what most of us call dragonflies) and *Callibaetis* mayflies, which are fairly large and show somewhat obvious segmented bodies. In many waters these bugs are present from early June to early September. At others there are intense hatches at various times. The fishes' IQs seem to go down by about half at those times, making them easier to catch. When a hatch isn't on, try using fairly natural-appearing flies. Unlike in streams and rivers, lake fish have plenty of time to scope out a fly and decide whether to eat it or not.

In scoping out a lake, look for the vegetation zones, which usually ring a lake at between 3 and 15 feet of depth; 2 feet or less of depth is not usually very productive. In many areas the trees and bushes grow right out to the water's edge, making backcasting difficult. Add to this the fact that fish like to accumulate on the deep side of a ledge (and a ledge is usually preceded by a steep bank), and wading out far enough to backcast is not possible without taking a dip. Roll casts work at those times for nymphs and emergers but will sink a dry fly pretty quickly. Backcasts, when possible, will shake water out of the fly, enhancing its flotation ability.

These conditions make float tube fishing a good idea. An angler in a float tube can position himself in deeper water and cast to the shore. But if a float tube is impractical, remember that fish tend to stack up near the inlets and particularly in front of outlets where food is concentrated. In those cases the angler can wade out a few feet and backcast parallel to the shore to avoid the vegetation, plopping a fly in those areas without too much trouble.

When nothing else is working in rivers, streams, or lakes, try a streamer, Woolly Buggers or Muddler Minnows. I've had good luck dead-drifting streamers and Woolly Buggers in medium to fast water or slow- or fast-stripping them through pools, deep holes, and of course lakes. These flies imitate small fish, and even tired fish have a hard time passing up such a large meal, the nutritional equivalent of about 5,000 mayflies.

One of my favorite tactics in moving water is to cast across fast water and let the water sweep the lure into an obstruction, something like a brush pile, downed tree, or large rock that is forcing the water back into the middle of the river. There is usually a buffer of slower water right in front of the obstruction, allowing the fish to cherry-pick other fish and bugs from the fast-moving current.

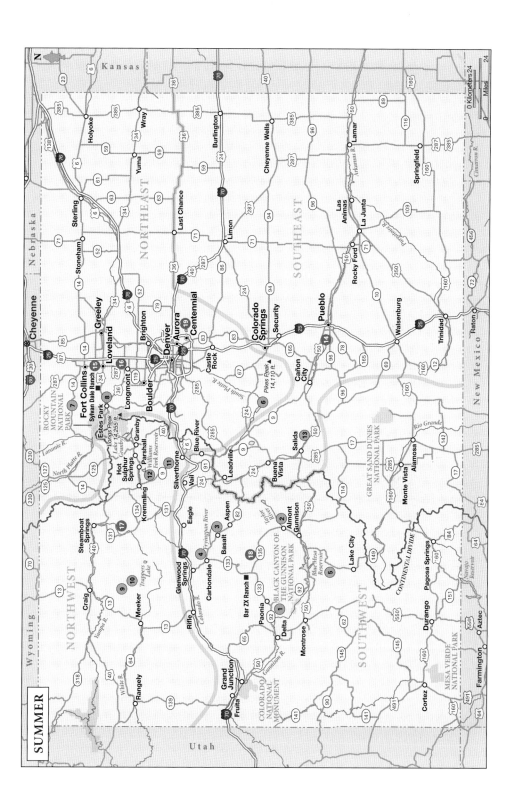

Muddler Minnows are usually heavily weighted and meant to be fished on or near the bottom. With muddlers and weighted Woolly Buggers in slower pocket water, it sometimes works to cast behind a rock, let it settle to the bottom, and give a few very short jerks.

While streamers are an option in summer fishing, it's in the fall that they really come into their own. See the seasonal information about fall fishing for year-round tactics, suggested streamer patterns, terminal tackle, and strategies for streamers. If there's anything more fun than streamer fishing, it's probably illegal.

SOUTHWEST REGION

1. GUNNISON RIVER IN GUNNISON GORGE

The 14-mile section of the Gunnison River in the Gorge runs between the boundary of the Black Canyon National Park upstream and Pleasure Park downstream, at the confluence with the North Fork of the Gunnison River east of the city of Delta, Colorado. Its location on the relatively warmer western slope, at an altitude of about 6,000 feet at the rim, makes it a true four-season fishery.

The Gunnison River in the Gunnison Gorge may well be one of the most difficult big waters to reach. It's accessible only by hiking one of four steep and sometimes difficult trails, ranging in length from 1.1 to 4.5 miles, with elevation changes of between 560 and 1,200 feet. In August 2010 a flash flood sent boulders down the steep sides of the canyon and rearranged some of those trails. Rock, mud, and gravel changed the banks and inundated some campgrounds. Since the slides were in a Wilderness Area, only a limited amount of work was done to clear them. The Colorado Division of Wildlife estimates that fish in only a 1.5-mile stretch might have been affected, but even these should rebound quickly.

If it rains, the roads become impassable to all but the most aggressive four-wheel drives. And the only road that goes all the way to the river, just west of the confluence with the North Fork, is canted enough to send a vehicle into the river when wet. Nevertheless, thousands of anglers make the trip every year.

It's not hard to understand why—with its staggering scenery and extremely high trout populations—this may well be the crown jewel of Colorado trout fishing.

Population

A 2005 fish census estimated an astounding average 7,000 brown trout per mile throughout its 14-mile length. Many of those fish are in the 15- to 18-inch range. The largest were 24 to 27 inches long. There was a smattering of rainbows present, but by 2012 the stocking of Hofer whirling disease (WD)–resistant rainbows should bring those numbers up quite a bit.

The Gunnison Gorge is worth hiring a guide the first time you fish it in order to learn the terrain. Why not take it easy, like these folks, until you get the lay of the land? JACK BRAUER

Flows

Water releases in May and June range from 300 cubic feet per second to more than 7,500 c.f.s. and can change quickly. Even in low-water years, the current is extremely strong, and water higher than midthigh can sweep an angler away. Flows at this location in excess of 500 c.f.s. are considered unsafe for wading. The average flow for a year's period is 300 to 400 c.f.s.

Access

Access to the four trailheads occurs primarily east on Falcon Valley Road from US 50, the junction a mile south of Olathe, to Peach Valley Road, which connects to all four trailheads. These trails all lead to the upper 7 miles of river in the gorge.

But there are two other ways to get to the river. One is to wade or float across the North Fork of the Gunnison above the confluence with the Gunnison at Pleasure Park, well marked on CO 92, about 12 miles east of Delta. The North Fork is often dewatered by irrigation in the summer and can be quite a bit lower than the main stem Gunnison. There is a 4-mile-long trail along the east bank of the river once you are across. The other method of access is to take CO 92 east out of Delta for 5 miles to H. 75 Dr. and stay on it until it reaches the main stem Gunnison south of the confluence with the North Fork Gunnison River at Confluence Park. The banks are more manageable on both sides of the river and allow greater access to the river. The river is wider and shallower in the first few miles above the confluence than upstream and is therefore more likely wadable.

Anglers are encouraged to wear a wading belt, have a wading staff, and wear studded felt or rubber soles for safety anywhere on the river.

Summer Strategy

Fishing the Gunnison Gorge in the summer, especially in the upper reaches of the river, is not a casual activity. I don't often suggest that anglers hire a guide or outfitter, but if I ever were going to recommend it, it would be for the upper gorge. One float trip would be all an angler needs to return on his or her own. There are simply too many variables to have much chance at a successful fishing experience your first time into the gorge. There is the flow to contend with, as well as unknown terrain along the river and possible crowding. Hiking down and camping for a couple of days is a better idea, but there are only a limited number of campsites along the river, and they are on a first-come, first-served basis.

Fortunately, there is another option—fish the river above the confluence. While brown trout predominate in the upper stretch of the river, there are also more rainbows in the relative flat water of this stretch, and they are quite likely some of the biggest fish in the gorge. Remember, you have to wade or float across to get to the east bank in this section, and the road to the west bank is nearly impassable and possibly dangerous when it rains. And remember, this is a jeep trail even in dry weather. That means a four-wheel-drive, high-clearance vehicle.

Tactics and Flies

Big water takes big equipment. To fish this stretch of the Gunnison, 9- to 10-foot six-weight or seven-weight rods, with a leader tapering to 3X thickness, are needed. It's a good idea to bring an extra rod and reel along.

With 7,000 brown trout per mile and many rainbows, Gunny Gorge is one of the crown jewels of Colorado trout fishing. Tim Romano

The premier event of the year is the giant salmon fly hatch, occurring when the water warms to 50 degrees. You can tell when the hatch starts going off by the cars driven by people in fishing vests speeding down the gravel roads toward the river.

The Gunnison Gorge hatch begins at Pleasure Park and moves upstream as the water temperature warms, usually just after the peak of runoff. The salmon fly is a type of large (2-inch-long) stonefly and like other stoneflies has a nymph stage wherein they crawl onto dry rocks and banks to shed their exoskeleton in early mornings before flying off to mature, mate, and begin laying eggs. Salmon flies can be in the air, but the time to fish dry flies is when they are laying their eggs. If the fish aren't hitting your dries, use a very large dark brown or black stonefly nymph. If they are hitting your dries, the takes can be ferocious, with big splashy strikes on top. Any flat-water eddies or slow areas against the bank, especially beneath streamside bushes and trees, are the target areas. When the hatch dies down, go deep into pools with 12-foot leaders and a lot of weight, or use a fast sinking line to get down to where the fish are eating. Unfortunately, a little luck is involved in catching this hatch. But that's the name of the game. The hatch begins in the middle of June and can last until mid-July or later.

For dry flies try an orange Stimulator #4 to #8 or a Royal Stimulator #4 to #8. For nymphs try a Kaufmann's Golden Stone #6 to #8. If your local fly shop doesn't have the flies in these large sizes, any shop within 25 miles of the Gunnison Gorge will stock them.

The next hatch is the caddis, which begins in mid-June and typically lasts until mid-September. There are several species of caddis in the gorge, and you'll see them continually during the day. The two predominant caddis species are the little black caddis, which hatches in June and July, and the great gray spotted caddis, which hatches from July to September.

Fish the larva pattern up and across, weighted so it's near the bottom through riffles, runs, and pocket water, and the emerger across and down, letting the fly lift at the end of the swing through slow water after the sun has gone down. After two or three casts, move downstream and try again. Fish the dry in slow water using short casts in the evening. Dry flies can be drifted as well as skated across the water to imitate egg layers.

Perfectflystore.com makes excellent patterns for gray spotted wing caddis, #10 to #12 and for the little black caddis, #16 to #18. If nothing else, take a look at their pictures, and buy something similar at your local shop. Green- and cream-colored Barr's Netbuilder Caddis #12 is a great imitation of the larval stage. LaFontaine's Sparkle Pupa Emerger is a killer pattern for this life stage.

While the salmon fly and caddis hatches are the predominate ones in the gorge, there is also a yellow Sally stonefly hatch from mid-June to mid-August; a green drake mayfly, a PMD, and a red quill mayfly hatch, all from early July to mid-August; and a BWO mayfly hatch in August and September.

The best fishing for PMDs starts around 9 a.m. and begins again in mid- to late afternoon into the evening. A light olive parachute pattern #16 will match the hatch. The drakes will hatch from the afternoon into the evening. Try a Wulff Green Drake #10 to #12. For the BWO try a Parawulff BWO dry fly, the Barr's BWO emerger and the Silver Copper John Nymph, all #16 to #20.

The river gets pretty choked with vegetation in slower spots late in the summer, so I suggest trying a bounce rig, which is becoming popular for weedy waters (it's actually a very old setup coming back into favor). It involves tying a tippet with three blood knots, leaving the tags tied 18 inches long. Two flies are attached to the top two tag lines and a weight to the last knot. This rig enables the weight to brush the weeds without snagging the line. It's kind of a pain to tie but so is rerigging every time you get snagged. It has the advantage of putting the flies downstream from the weights and strike indicator, which is less likely to spook the fish.

2. Taylor River

This section of the Taylor River begins below Taylor Park Reservoir in the upper Gunnison Basin and runs 20 miles southwest to join the East River at Almont, where the two rivers join to become the Gunnison River. The Taylor River runs through a canyon, becoming a series of riffles, runs, tumbling rapids, and pools. The town of Gunnison is on US 50, about 3 hours west of Pueblo. From Denver take US 285 southwest to US 50, and head west on US 50 to Gunnison. Almont is 11 miles north of Gunnison on CO 135.

If ever a river had a split personality, it would be the Taylor. The upper 0.4 of a mile (a true four-season fishery for the mildly insane angler willing to brave the winter weather) is a meadow river with monster, worldly-wise trout, mostly rainbows. Anglers say of the Taylor that the trout are born with master's degrees and within a few years have a couple of PhDs. Of all the tailwaters the upper stretch of the Taylor River, which is catch-and-release, is the most technical but ultimately the most rewarding, producing three state records for rainbows since 2002. The most recent was a 40¼-inch football with a girth of 29 inches.

The lower river is checkered with private property and is a high-running, wild haven for brown trout, often in the 10- to 15-inch range. The qualitative difference is that the upper 0.4 mile is a nice, usually slow run of water that has millions of mysis shrimp pumped into it from the reservoir on a regular basis. The fish there gorge on the shrimp and don't have to work very hard to eat. The lower river is just too tumultuous for the trout to typically grow to any great size and has just the normal, or a slightly better, number of insects to feed the trout.

> ### PRO TIP
>
> Dragonfly Anglers' Rod Cesario suggests finding a spot where you can wade across the river to fish from the opposite bank and thus get away from the crowds. Hopefully, you'll find fish that have done the same thing —tried to get away from the crowds.

Population

I haven't seen any stream population surveys on either the upper or lower river, but the pounds-per-acre measure is probably the highest in the state. Creel-census surveys on the lower river are not particularly high, not in the least the result of inexperienced anglers stopping and fishing at random

Until the water calms down in mid-August, some of the best fishing in the Taylor River can be found in the pocket water. RUSSELL MILLER

spots along the river in the middle of the day, then reporting few fish caught. If planning was ever necessary, it would be on the Taylor River, upper or lower section. This river is WD-positive.

Flows
The Taylor River runoff/release from the dam typically peaks earlier (in May) than most tailwaters but unlike other rivers remains fairly clear because the streambed is mostly rock. The historic peak high is 850 cubic feet per second. The riverbed's gradient drops continuously until a couple of miles above Almont and makes wading intimidating until mid-August, when the flow normally hits about 300 c.f.s.

Access
There are many places to park along the public access portion (11 miles) of the lower river and quite a few on the upper 0.4 mile. The problem with parking is that areas where you can see the river from the road fill up quickly, as does the adjacent stretch of water. But there are many fine places to fish that

can't be seen from the roadway. Avoid the urge to jump on the first stretch of open water and instead spend a day scouting the river, particularly for pocket waters and wading accesses—it will pay off. The tailwater is restricted to flies and lures only, catch-and-release.

Summer Strategy

Due to the Jekyll and Hyde nature of the tailwater and the lower 19.6 miles of the river, two very different strategies are called for. On the tailwater's 0.4 mile, if you are serious about fishing the summer season, you will first need to deal with the crowds. Gear up early and find an open, 50-foot stretch of bank to cast from. Stream etiquette on crowded days requires the angler to stay on the bank or near the bank and not wade into the river. On less crowded days, usually in spring, fall, and definitely in the winter, there's more latitude in this regard. In the summer anglers are not shy about reminding an offending angler of the proper etiquette.

If the crowds aren't particularly bad, try to find a fish and cast to it, using a good pair of polarized sunglasses. Often the fish will be in front of rocks, enjoying the hydraulic buffer. But look the river over—the fish are there. I once spooked a big rainbow in about a foot of water against a slightly under-cut bank. Any fly must be nailed right on the nose of the trout. But these fish reportedly shy away from split shot and even bead head flies, because they've come to associate them with getting caught.

Strategy on the lower river for the first part of the summer involves finding and fishing pocket water. By mid- to late July, a period that incidentally coincides with the green drake hatch, the lower water creates a lot more areas and opportunities to fish. Rod Cesario, owner of Dragonfly Anglers in Crested Butte, calls this hatch "phenomenal" and suggests anglers go geared for the big drakes. Even if the drakes aren't present, caddis and pale morning duns will be around in July and August.

Tactics and Flies

The ideal rod for the tailwater stretch is a 9-foot five or six-weight with a 9-foot leader tapering to 5X. Some anglers who are very successful use leaders 14 feet long with a fluorocarbon tippet. To get the fly down to fish level, use dull green-colored split shot and nongold bead head flies. Since mysis shrimp are flushed out of the reservoir all year long, a number of shrimp sizes are recommended. For colors stick with a white to translucent, with a touch of pink or red to simulate an organism wounded in the dam release tubes, such as Palm's Mysis Shrimp #16. The fish don't generally move much to take a shrimp, so any movement by the fish, no matter how slight, should be a signal to set the hook. In fact, they take flies the same way, so you can see how important good polarized sunglasses are. Drop a midge pattern, such as the Rojo #16 to #22 in red, black, or olive or the WD 40 #18 to #22 gray black or brown, off the bend in the hook to double your chances. If a good presentation with your flies isn't working, change flies. The only hatch that routinely draws these big fish to the surface seems to be green drakes. Try a Wulff's Green Drake #10 to #12, and drop a Crown Jewell Green Drake #12 nymph in a 2-fly setup. The drakes normally hatch from mid-July to the end of August but can, with warm weather, hatch much later. Blue-winged olive mayflies will begin hatching in September. Or try an emerger/nymph setup with Barr's Wet Emerger PMD #18 to #22 on top and an RS-2 #18 to #22 below.

If the fish in the tailwater have double doctorate degrees, the fish in the lower river are freshmen in college. Except that they are, well ... brown trout and therefore kind of unpredictable. They are hatch oriented and tend to be more active in the morning and evening. The caddis hatch in the lower river begins in May and lasts until mid-September and possibly later. The PMD hatch runs from July to September, and the green drake hit in mid-July through August and later. That puts a lot of insects in the water and makes for some confusion. A good selection of flies representing each of these insects is critical.

3. FRYINGPAN RIVER

The 14-mile stretch of the Fryingpan River—a true four-season fishery, given that the entire length stays ice free most of the year—begins at Ruedi Reservoir dam and ends at its confluence with the Roaring Fork River at the town of Basalt, about midway between Aspen and Glenwood Springs. Glenwood Springs is about 2 hours west of Denver on I-70.

Several years ago, when I was fishing the catch-and-release section of the "Pan," as the river is known locally, I watched a guide tell his client to cast a black Woolly Bugger right at the back of a bushel-basket-size stone in the river and let the fly sit. The first cast missed, so he told the client to try again; this time he was right on target. The guide said to give it a little jerk. What turned out to be a nearly 8-pound brown hit the bugger and then, after only

An angler helps his "buddy" land a big fish on the Fryingpan River. A helping hand is often necessary to keep a big fish from breaking the line. TIM ROMANO

about 30 seconds of fighting, promptly rolled over. That told me two things: that fish was almost always there, and it had been caught so many times it had learned to not waste much energy fighting.

Population

A 2010 population survey at the Baetis Bridge (the first bridge below the dam) estimated 1,114 brown trout and 425 rainbow trout per acre at that survey site, with 525 browns and 134 rainbows larger than 14 inches per mile in the same area. Hofer strain rainbows have been stocked in the Fryingpan for 4 years.

An area called the Toilet Bowl, just below the dam, holds trout in the 10- to 15-pound range. The presence of mysis shrimp from the reservoir explains the size of these fish. The upper 2 miles has catch-and-release, fly-and-lure-only restrictions.

Flows

Another plus for the "Pan" is that flows are predictable and fishable in normal precipitation years, except for a short runoff peak in early June. However, the terrain downstream produces slightly faster water for most of the season.

Access

Many anglers fish the upper mile, given its easy access and parking, but the fish populations in the second mile are only a little less than the upper mile, and fewer anglers are on that water. Access to the lower river is plentiful, with more than 8 miles open to the public between the town of Basalt and the 2 miles of catch-and-release water below the dam. There is usually parking adjacent to the public water in the lower stretch, but if you get there late, it may require some hiking. The river, particularly the upper mile, gets incredibly crowded during the summer weekends. The crowds thin out and the fish are slightly less finicky once you get away from the first mile below the dam or if you go in the middle of the week.

Summer Strategy

The fish, sometimes described as PhD fish, are picky. Success requires exact duplication of the type, size, and color of any hatching insects. You need to be able to cast directly to the fish and float your line without drag.

When determining how to fish the Pan during the summer, you should divide the river into two segments: the catch-and-release section and the rest of the river down to Basalt. As stated earlier, fish in the catch-and-release section are heavily fished and very picky. Precision is the key. Sight-fishing is possible in much of that section, as it is dominated by runs and pools. The fish are not particularly spooked by the presence of humans, but it is strongly believed that they are by strike indicators. So a white-tipped fly line is a good idea; if that is not possible, use a light-colored piece of floating yarn secured high on the leader.

When you can't sight-fish, all the spots that look like good holding or feeding lies probably hold a fish and often a big one.

Tactics and Flies

If you're going to fish the first mile below the dam, try a Mysis Shrimp pattern, #14 to #16. When they are plentiful in the water, the fish gorge on them.

By the slackening of runoff in June, both pale morning duns (there is actually some debate about whether these insects are PMDs or another subspecies called pink alberts or pink ladies—the locals call them PMDs) and caddis are hatching. PMDs will last until September, and caddis often into October. The PMDs begin hatching about noon but can be fished effectively all day long. The adults are more pink than yellow and should be fished in #14 to #20. An effective dry-fly pattern is A.K.'s Melon Quill, standard hackle or parachute style. For nymphing a Pheasant Tail Nymph #16 to #20 is always a good choice.

When caddis are hatching the fish are more forgiving of

> ## PRO TIP
>
> The lower stretches of river from Basalt to mile marker 6 are overlooked by anglers, despite the great fishing and hatches. According to Kirk Webb of Taylor Creek Fly Shop, if you want to avoid angling pressure, this is the area to focus on.

size and color, although an angler should have flies from #12 to #18 in a variety of colors. To imitate adult flies, use an Elkhair Caddis style, and then a variety of different styles for larvae and emergers. If you can find a Colorado Caddis (it's a soft black hackle with a fuzzy yellow body), it's still a great fly for emerging caddis. They aren't in many shops, but some wholesalers still have them in back stock. If one fly doesn't work, keep trying others.

The green drake mayfly hatch may be the best on the Pan. It certainly is for dry-fly fishing anglers. These hatches begin in early July and are intermittent until mid-September. The adults will be on the water early in the morning laying eggs—and early means about an hour after sunrise. The adults tend to hatch throughout the day, particularly when the sun is off the water. But the best hatches are toward the evening. Later in the summer when the water begins to warm, work the riffles, where trout hang out to get oxygen. In this case use a bushy, high floater such as the Stimulator.

A standard or Parachute Adams #10 to #12 is excellent for fishing the green drake hatch on the surface in low-light situations, even though they are gray. Also try a green Stimulator #10 to #12 for drakes. The flies are a lot brighter green than the insects but seem to work anyway. There are many patterns that effectively imitate the green drake dun or spinner, however.

The Crown Jewel Green Drake #12 is probably the best (certainly the most realistic) nymph pattern. But an olive Hare's Ear #10 to #12 will work well if you can't find a Crown Jewel Green Drake. Any fly shop can order the Crown Jewel Drakes from Idylwilde, but you have to buy a dozen. They're worth it.

Fishing the lower 12 miles early in the summer, even after runoff, is more challenging physically because the gradient is steeper, and with a number of side streams dumping into it, it is faster water. Finding feeding and resting lies requires a bit of scouting because the conditions are continually changing. The same hatches are present as in the catch-and-release stretch, but the timing may be a little different. A bonus to this is the presence of stoneflies, goldens in much of this stretch, with some salmon flies in the first 5 miles up the canyon.

Poxyback Golden Stone Nymph imitations #8 to #14 will work where the insects are present, and black or brown Kaufmann's Stonefly Nymphs sizes #6 to #12 are effective for the salmon fly hatches.

By August the water has usually dropped to about 150 cubic feet per second and by early September to about 100 c.f.s., opening up most of the lower river to easy wading. With the 38- to 40-degree water coming out of the reservoir, it never warms up a lot but does a bit in the middle of the day. At those times terrestrials—hoppers, ants, and beetles—are effective if nothing else is working. They're always a good bet and will stir a fish off the bottom in the heat of day. And of course, as the fishing guide mentioned above, you can always try a streamer or a Woolly Bugger, either retrieved quickly through a run or pool or let sink to the bottom in a slow spot, then stripped or dead-drifted. Bigger fish are always on the lookout for a big, easy meal.

4. ROARING FORK RIVER

With headwaters at 12,000 feet in the Hunter/Fryingpan Wilderness, the Roaring Fork River flows 70 miles through alpine meadows, canyons, and the red-rock foothills of the trendy and bustling Roaring Fork Valley, home of Aspen, Colorado, to a confluence with the Colorado River at Glenwood Springs. Given the presence of the Fryingpan and Colorado Rivers, this area may be the best four-season fishing destination in the state.

Unlike the Fryingpan River, the Roaring Fork is a freestone stream and subject to, depending upon snowpack, very high and difficult fishing waters anytime from April to June.

Population

The most recent fish stream census on the Roaring Fork River estimated that in a 2.5-mile stretch below the town of Basalt there were 2,300 brown trout and 3,000 whitefish. As of the late 1990s, whirling disease had all but wiped out the rainbow trout population in that reach. But this stretch of river is decent rainbow habitat, and with the stocking of the Hofer variety (WD-resistant) rainbows well under way, there should be a resurgence of the rainbow population in a short time.

Flows

In 2010 the Roaring Fork River at its confluence with the Colorado River peaked in May at 1,200 cubic feet per second and in June at 9,000, then dropped in August to 800 c.f.s. Above Basalt it peaked at about 1,200 c.f.s. all the way to below Aspen at the same flow. By August the flows were at 200 to 300 c.f.s.

Access

Because of its length and varied conditions and the fact that this is a highly developed suburban corridor, the most valuable piece of advice for the out-of-town angler is to buy an access map. There are numerous fly shops in the area, and several excellent maps are available. Some of the access points are obvious, but many are not. Without a map it can become maddeningly frustrating trying to get on the river. The private property along the river is very well marked. Don't drive around blindly and expect much friendly assistance at any place but the fly shops.

Summer Strategy

For fishing purposes the river should be divided into three sections.

The first is the 14-mile stretch between the confluence with the Colorado River in Glenwood Springs upstream to Carbondale/Crystal River. The river here is wider and flatter than it is upstream, and though the flow is higher, wading is possible except at the 2- to 3-week peak of runoff. The river channel appears featureless, but there are many seams and depressions and submerged rocks for holding areas. The biggest fish in the river take advantage of that. And many of those fish are rainbows that come up from the Colorado River. Every insect hatch on the river begins at the Colorado and works its way upstream.

This lower section is also rated a Gold Medal Water by the Colorado Division of Wildlife—the highest rating in terms of number and size of fish—and is restricted to fly and lure fishing. But anglers are allowed to keep two fish per day of 16 inches or larger. This is unusual on a Gold Medal Water, but it speaks to the quality of the fishing. There are also 12 access areas in this stretch, on both sides of the river, but don't count on the locals to give you directions.

PRO TIP

Kirk Webb of Taylor Creek Fly Shop says, "Many of the fish will hold suspended in the water column, making dry/dropper/dropper rigs often the most successful. We often fish a large foam-bodied attractor dry-trailed by a Tungsten Prince and a BWO nymph."

The next (middle) section begins at Carbondale and extends 12 miles upstream to Basalt. It is similar in structure to the lower section but with a little faster water due to elevation change. Wading might be more difficult around runoff. There are fewer public access points in this stretch, but there is 3 miles of public access on the north side of the river adjacent to Basalt. It's often crowded, and since the locals and even fishing guides can be territorial, don't spoil your experience by trying to force your way into a crowd. Just move to another spot. The middle river section is also fly-and-lure-only water and allows the same take as the lower section—two fish over 16 inches per day. The river course is a little more varied, with a few islands, longer runs, and deeper pools. Whitefish, particularly, love these holes, and if an angler can get a nymph (any nymph) down in the holes, he or she can take the limit home and smoke them for a very

Andrew Zentner holds a big rainbow he caught in the Roaring Fork River on a green drake. RUSSELL MILLER

tasty feed. Whitefish don't have the mojo of trout, but they can be fun and are easier to catch than trout. I've caught quite a few and couldn't tell it wasn't a trout until I got it almost in.

The 21-mile upper section of the river extends from Basalt to Aspen and is quite different from the lower two sections. The gradient is steeper, and the river channel is narrower and is mostly riffles with a few runs and pools. The closer to Aspen, the faster the water becomes. The fish are smaller—mostly brown and brook trout—but they are much more numerous than in the lower sections. Almost the entire stretch is accessible from the Rio Grande Trail that runs to within about 3 miles of Basalt. The water stays cooler in this stretch, and hatches come off later in the summer, making it a good area to fish when the heat in the valley puts the fish down during the day.

Tactics and Flies

The hatches on the Roaring Fork are nearly identical to the nearby Fryingpan River, with one exception—stoneflies have a major presence in the Roaring Fork, as the long riffles make for excellent stonefly hatcheries. Two types are present—large black/brown insects and golden stones. The big, dark stoneflies often come off during runoff in late May or early June, while the smaller golden stones hatch throughout the summer. For the giant dark stones, use a Hoffman Stone Fly Nymph, sizes #8 to #12. For topside fishing there are large, dark flies called Royal Stimulators, sizes #10 to #12, that work well for these adult insects. For a golden stonefly hatch, any of the plastic Stone Nymphs, sizes #10 to #16, should work well. Choose one with the antennae, legs, and short tail protuberances. These are sometimes part of the fly's body or are often rubber legs. Either should work well. For the adults yellow, orange, and green Stimulators, sizes #12 to #16, are effective. I think it's fair to say the fish aren't as particular on the Fork as on the Pan. But it's still a good idea to have a decent selection of flies available, in terms of size and color, whether for stoneflies or for any other insect that might be on the water.

When water is high and fast, just cast into slow areas along the banks. If there's no vegetation on the banks, it's not even necessary to get in the water. But if you do, be careful. Test the depth and current with a stick, and be careful on the smooth stones under the water. The Fork is well known for its slippery stones.

As the runoff clears and starts slowing down, both pale morning duns and caddis hatch. The PMDs will last until September and caddis often into October. The PMDs begin hatching about noon but can be fished effectively all day long. The adults are more pink than yellow and should be fished in #14 to #18. An effective dry fly pattern is A.K.'s Melon Quill, standard hackle or parachute style. For nymphing, a Pheasant Tail Nymph #16 to #18 is always a good choice.

The green drake mayfly hatch may be the best hatch on the Fork. It certainly is for dry-fly fishing anglers. These hatches begin in early July and are intermittent until mid-September, moving up the river continually until mid-September. And like the stoneflies the fish get a little crazy with those big morsels available. They are not sipping tiny mayflies; they're gobbling like hogs at the trough. Later in the summer when the water begins to warm, it's a good idea for fishermen to work the riffles where trout hang out to get oxygen. In this case, use a bushy, high floater such as a Stimulator.

A standard or Parachute Adams #10 to #12 or green Stimulator #10 to #12 for drakes are excellent for fishing the green drake hatch on the surface. The Stimulators are a lot brighter green than the insects but work anyway. There are many patterns that effectively imitate the green drake, however. An olive Hare's Ear #10 to #12 will certainly work well.

If an angler has to pick one fly to fish with on the Roaring Fork, it would be the Tan Elkhair Caddis. Caddis flies are present from the middle of June until October, with periodically prolific hatches. The species of caddis varies, but both dry flies and Soft Hackle wet flies, such as the Colorado Caddis or Breadcrusts, are killer during hatches. Patterns that imitate caddis larvae work better when the hatch is off because during the hatch the fish are looking up, not down.

5. Lake Fork of the Gunnison River

The headwaters of the Lake Fork of the Gunnison River are in the basin below Red Cloud and Handies Peak, above Lake City, which is about 50 miles southwest of Gunnison. The river flows north through canyons and steep valleys in the upper section into Lake San Cristobal, then through Lake City and north through ranch country into Blue Mesa Reservoir.

The Lake Fork, as it's known locally, is one of my favorite places to fish. I learned the joys of fishing the green drake hatch there and have since consistently caught big fish there. A 5-mile stretch of the river through Bureau of Land Management property has had very nice habitat features built into it, greatly increasing the health of the fishery since the time when it was primarily grazing land. About 14 miles of public access is available on the section between Lake City and Blue Mesa Reservoir.

Every type of water imaginable can be found at the various public access spots, from rapids and riffles to long slow runs and deep pools.

The best thing about the Lake Fork is the lack of fishing pressure. Comparable to many other spots in Colorado with quality fishing, the Lake Fork often almost seems deserted.

Population

The river is whirling disease positive, and rainbow trout reproduction declined from 1998 to 2008. But the Hofer strain of WD-resistant rainbows has been stocked since 2009. Brown trout make up about 80 percent of the fish sampled, rainbows the other 20. The sampling estimated that there are 23 browns and 4 rainbows longer than 14 inches per surface acre of water. I've caught an 18-inch brownie directly adjacent to the Gate Campground and saw a 24-inch brown caught under the bridge just upstream from there. There are big fish in this river if the angler is patient.

Flows

Runoff high flows reach between 1,500 and 2,000 cubic feet per second in early June but taper off fairly quickly, dropping to 500 c.f.s. in early July, then consistently downward to 100 to 200 c.f.s. and lower through the fall, winter, and spring. The ideal flow for fishing is between 400 and 500 c.f.s., with the water warming during the days below 400 c.f.s. to temperatures that push fish activity to the morning and evening.

In the habitat-improved sections of the Lake Fork of the Gunnison River, stoneflies and green drakes are important as the water begins to clear after runoff. NANCY MORRELL

Access

Most of the action is on the lower river, with a short stretch above the Gate Campground. A 5-mile stretch below the Gates (two very prominent vertical geologic structures) is private, and if you try to float it, you might be decapitated by a steel cable stretched across the river at the upper boundary of the private water. Below that stretch, which occurs right as CO 149 comes off a long hill and turns south, paralleling the river to Lake City, CR 25 turns north, and public access begins about ¼ mile north. Because the landowner stocks the river with trophy fish throughout his 5 miles, some of the best fishing begins right at the border to the private land. Don't worry about trespassing. The landowner marks his property right at the property line.

From that property line downstream to Blue Mesa Reservoir is all public access. The river before Blue Mesa Reservoir is a narrow canyon with cascades and large pools and many places to park.

Summer Strategy

The thing to do on the Lake Fork is to get there while runoff is high and clear but dropping and to fish the habitat improvement areas or, if you are really patient, the upstream areas (where the fish are more difficult to catch). My first experience on the Lake Fork was in high water (600 to 700 c.f.s.) and fishing with a streamer, swinging it into the current upstream so the current forced it along the face of brush piles. Fish stack up there and cherry-pick the water for edible morsels floating by. I caught several 15- to 16-inch rainbows and browns using a floating minnow pattern. When I returned a couple of weeks later, the stoneflies and green drakes were hatching, and the fishing was so good I drove the 50 miles into Gunnison to buy a net. I usually try to unhook trout without taking them from the water, but these fish were so large that I couldn't do it.

> **PRO TIP**
>
> Fishing with a Golden Stonefly Nymph is always a good idea on the Lake Fork, according to Oscar Marks of Gunnison River Fly Shop.

As the water gets lower and warmer, the best fishing can be had either earlier in the day or later, about half an hour after the sun goes off the water until dark.

Tactics and Flies

Golden stoneflies, caddis flies, green and gray drakes, and pale morning duns all begin hatching in mid-June. Although the caddis have been around since mid-April, they pretty much disappear during the peak of runoff. Most of the action at the end of runoff will be nymph, larvae, and emerger patterns. By mid-July most of the concentrated hatches will be over, but these insects are around well into August. Bead Head Hare's Ears #8 to #10 in olive or gray will take fish looking for the drake nymphs. Bead Head Prince Nymphs #10 to #18 are effective for caddis larvae and emergers.

As the water comes down, fish will take dry flies. Again, a 2-fly rig using an emerger/nymph or an emerger/cripple will work best.

NORTHEAST REGION

6. South Platte River in Eleven Mile Canyon

This stretch of the South Platte River runs through a scenic canyon below the dam on Eleven Mile Reservoir, ending near Lake George on US 24, about 30 miles west of Colorado Springs. It features long, slow meanders; riffle/run/pool complexes; deep, lakelike pools; and cascades.

The river in Eleven Mile Canyon will always hold a special place in my heart, partly because it was where I caught my first trout on a fly I had tied. A fisherman nearby asked me what I was using. I showed him, and he said, "Oh, yeah, a snow midge emerger. Good choice." Well, I'd thought it was an oversized mayfly nymph with a little loop wing, but I just nodded knowingly. It was April, and there was indeed snow on the banks. I learned that these are among the largest midges found in Colorado, being almost the size of an Alaska mosquito.

Population

The upper catch-and-release section (stretching about 2 miles downstream from the dam) has one of the heaviest concentrations of rainbow trout in the entire state. A fish population survey in 2005 estimated there were more than 3,500 trout per mile in the catch-and-release stretch. Though 15- to 18-inch rainbows are not uncommon, more will be in the 12- to 14-inch range. They are so healthy that they seem much bigger when you are trying to land one. Surprisingly, rainbows are now populating the lower, nonrestricted 8 miles of river—something of a miracle, given that the entire South Platte River system has been hit hard by whirling disease. In the past 20 years, almost no rainbows have reproduced successfully in the entire river system—except in Eleven Mile Canyon.

The only blot on the fishery is that New Zealand mud snails have shown up there. These little buggers are hell on fisheries because they eat the same thing as insects and, with no natural predators present, reproduce exponentially. Boots and waders must be cleaned to keep the snails from spreading.

Flows

While the average flow for the river is 150 to 200 cubic feet per second, dam releases raise the flow to unsafe and unfishable levels in early June but only for a few weeks. Generally, at this location, faster than 300 c.f.s. is considered unsafe for wading.

Access

There is plenty of access to the river along the road in the lower 8 miles of river from parking lots and pull-offs on the road. In the upper 2 miles, parking is at a premium, so arrive early or plan on a hike. It's a good idea to get there early anyway, because fishing guides will get there early and camp on the best sections of the river for the whole day. It's bad etiquette to move into an occupied spot, but the river is wide enough in many places that the far bank can be fished without interfering with anyone.

Summer Strategy

The presence of rainbows changes the strategy from most other places in Colorado because rainbows are opportunistic daytime feeders. Of course, any noticeable hatch should be fished accordingly, but unlike brown trout rainbows will feed when not much is going on hatchwise. The only time I've seen the 'bows turn off in Eleven Mile Canyon was in July, and they were actually grazing on midge larva on the rocks and nothing else. The trout were acting almost like suckers. All over the river the trout had become bottom feeders.

Midges are so thick in the canyon that, unlike many places where the tiny bugs become minor sources of food during the summer, they're always worth a try. I've caught rainbows and browns both, using Peach Eggs and Worms patterns.

These are not the PhD you'll find in many tailwaters—yet. But they're dumbest in the early spring and get smarter as the season goes along. In unusually warm summers the water temperatures never get significantly warmer: In normal years water is released over the dam, but in droughts it comes off the bottom of the 135-foot reservoir, so the stream stays nice and cool.

Tactics and Flies

For the little yellow stonefly stragglers still around at the tail end of runoff, try the Poxyback Yellow Sally #16 as a nymph and tan Stimulator #16 as a dry.

Caddis begin hatching in May and continue into September. The best time to fish is afternoon and evening.

For caddis larvae use cream, tan, and green patterns, such as the Buckskin #16 to #20, Olive Caddis Nymph #14 to #18, or Barr's Netbuilder Caddis #12 to #16. For emergers try LaFontaine's Sparkle Caddis Pupa #14 to #18 or the Yuba Pupa #14 to #16, depending upon what the bugs are doing. If it's quiet, use the larvae patterns. If there is a major hatch on, use the emergers because fish

PRO TIP

There are two tunnels on the road up the canyon. The stretch of water just below the last tunnel and a few hundred yards upstream is where I've done the best. Just above this stretch are a series of cascades, and above those there is about half a mile of meadow water that I always fish as soon I quit catching fish in the tunnel area.

can catch more of the emergers under water. Once they hit the surface, the bugs launch themselves into the air. If you want to use dry flies, such as the Elkhair Caddis tan or green #14 to #18 or the Clown Shoe Caddis green or brown #14 to #18, wait until the insects are returning to lay their eggs and die.

Fishing caddis emergers is fun because fish hit them hard. The bugs are very quick on their way to the surface. Cast up and across, with plenty of line slack, then either dead-drift or high-stick (my preference) for 15 to 25 feet downstream. Then hold the rod at 45 degrees to let the current lift the fly up in the water column; 75 percent of the strikes will come in the first 12 inches of liftoff.

The PMD hatch begins in early June and trails off in September. The best times to fish PMDs are early morning and evening or when it's cloudy or shadows fall upon the water.

Weighted PMD nymphs should be dead-drifted, and unweighted Pheasant Tail Nymphs #16 to #18 and Barr's PMD Emerger #16 to #18 can also be fished as cripples or dead insects on or just under the surface effectively.

In Eleven Mile Canyon use a dry on top and a midge dropper or a nymph/emerger on top with a midge dropper. I do this when the fly I'm using isn't drawing much attention. It usually works, with a fish taking the midge on the dropper.

Great midge patterns are the Rojo Midge #18 to #24 in red and black, Tungsten Midge, Brassie #18 to #22, Black Beauty #18 to #24, and the Jujubee #18 to #24.

The river gets pretty choked with vegetation in slower spots late in the summer, so I suggest trying a bounce rig, which is becoming popular for weedy waters.

7. Cache La Poudre River

The Cache La Poudre River canyon begins 10 miles northwest of Fort Collins and about a mile west of US 287 on CO 14. The name means "powder cache" in French, and legend has it that a group of French trappers buried a powder cache in the canyon in the early 1800s. The river begins in Rocky Mountain National Park and runs 70 miles before reaching the flatlands and private property. Throughout its length, every conceivable type of streambed structure can be found, from waterfalls and rapids to meadowlike, meandering stream cuts, with riffle, pool, and run complexes.

From bottom to top this is one of the most beautiful canyons in the entire state. For the past 20 years, I have worked this river more than all the other places I have fished combined.

Population

According to surveys, the highest numbers of large fish in the Cache La Poudre occur in a stretch called Indian Meadows. Indeed, the 2006 National Fly Fishing Championship was held in this 5-mile length of river.

A few years ago (and I'll swear this on a stack of Bibles), I approached one big Indian Meadows pool that had a large rock in the middle of it. From the high bank on the south side of the river, I saw a fish about 2 feet long holding not far from the rock. It saw me move, however, and immediately flitted to safety under the rock. To my knowledge no one has caught a Poudre fish that large in recent memory.

The river's rainbow population was decimated by whirling disease in the 1990s. And while brown trout have largely filled many of the habitat niches historically occupied by rainbows, given the new strain of WD–resistant rainbows, this picture should change.

Flows

As a true, undammed, freestone river draining a thousand square miles of mountains, the runoff can reach 2,000 and even 3,000 cubic feet per second quite a way up the canyon, making the entire river dangerous and unfishable till well into July. More normally, the river peaks at about 1,500 c.f.s. in early June and begins to be fishable in mid- to late June.

Jessie Wyard holds a beautiful brown trout caught in the Cache La Poudre. Summer fishing can be tricky during multiple hatches, but caddis are always a good bet. RUSSELL MILLER

Access

Wading access is extensive, but many of the pullouts are small, holding only one to two vehicles. In the summer these spots get filled early. Most camp-grounds, picnicking sites, and boat put-ins have designated parking spots for anglers. There is some private property far up the canyon where both banks are off limits, but it's well marked and nothing to worry about. While most of the river is open to the public, parking can be a problem in the upper river. Heading up the canyon early will help avoid a long hike to fish.

Summer Strategy

With this much river to choose from, picking a place to fish would seem difficult, but there are two areas that are fly and lure only—the first about 20 miles up the canyon from Pingree Park bridge up to the town of Rustic and the second from Black Hollow Creek near the old fishing hatchery up to Big Bend Campground.

There are plenty of fish in the entire river, so if you see a spot that looks good, give it a try. The lower 10 miles of river have very heavy rafting traffic most of the summer, so it's probably a good idea to plan on driving at least that far early in the summer season.

About 40 miles up the canyon is the Big South trailhead. At this point the river turns south, away from CO 14. You can fish this segment by following the Big South Trail, but the terrain is steep, and wading is difficult, if not hazardous. To get to the upper river, where conditions are better, continue on CO 14 for about 10 miles west to Forest Road 156—the turnoff to Long Draw Reservoir—and drive an additional 15 miles on a gravel road. There is a parking lot just before you reach the reservoir that allows access to the headwaters, which lie in a high altitude meadow with a flatter gradient and trails down both sides of the river. There's even a bridge to cross over the river.

The Poudre is joined by Long Draw Creek, which drains the reservoir and keeps flows in that section of river high enough to support healthy populations of rainbow, brown, brook, and cutthroat trout, making it possible for anglers to get a grand slam of trout fishing. The cutts can get to be 16 inches or larger. Flows remain high until mid- to late August but are manageable after the middle of the month. Above the confluence with Long Draw Creek, the Poudre is fishable weeks earlier. The fish are plentiful but on the small side, averaging 10 to 12 inches. There is open camping along FR 156 and a campground at the reservoir. Consider camping overnight to avoid the drive up and back down the canyon, allowing at least one full day of fishing.

> **PRO TIP**
>
> Fish August and September with a Parachute Hopper #10 to #14 on top, trailed by a Kiwi Beetle.

Tactics and Flies

Talking tactics on a 70-mile stretch of river is tricky. First of all, remember that hatch dates are relative. They typically begin downstream when the water temperature rises to a certain level, then move upstream. But different insects hatch at different temperatures. And since the river is all but blown out by runoff year after year for weeks at a time, we'll consider the summer season starting as runoff tapers off and the water clears.

If you absolutely have to fish during or right after runoff, consider fishing stonefly nymphs and caddis larvae along the banks. They must be weighted to give the fish a little more time to see and chase them. By some coincidence these are the two patterns I've had the best luck with on the Poudre, and not just during runoff. But they are critical during runoff. Stonefly nymphs begin moving during runoff and will hatch and lay eggs before it is over. Caddis are active subsurface for a long time before they hatch, and the fast water knocks a lot of larvae loose.

I've fished the Poudre perhaps 200 times over 20-plus years, from April through November, mornings and evenings during the summer, midday in the spring and fall, and I've never seen the kind of wave or blanket hatches that are common on many other trout rivers. I'm not saying they don't happen, just that I never witnessed any. From June through September what's more typical is that there will be several types of insects over the water at the same time. From June through August these might include caddis (four subspecies), green drake mayflies, red quill mayflies, pale morning duns, and both large and small stoneflies. It can be maddening trying to figure out what, if anything, the fish are eating. Because the brown trout on the Poudre get 90-plus percent of their food subsurface, it's a strong argument for a 2-nymph rig. Double fly rigs tend to foul-hook a fighting fish or tangle themselves on casts, but if you want to catch fish, they are the way to go.

As I said earlier, I usually just use Caddis Larvae #12 to #14, with cream or green bodies. The Buckskin Nymph #14 to #18 is an excellent caddis larvae imitation, and large, Dark Brown or Golden Stone patterns #8 to #12 are effective. I like the molded plastic with realistic rubber legs because real stonefly nymphs have a shiny body and rubbery legs.

The most rewarding and simple time to fish is during August and into September, when the fish key on terrestrials. Beetle patterns such as the Kiwi Beetle #14 to #16 are particularly effective because the pine beetle infestation in that area of Colorado puts a lot of bugs on the water. But grasshopper patterns are great and will draw a lethargic fish off the bottom. Don't be afraid to plop these flies noisily on the water. It tickles a brown trout's interest and reduces its wariness.

The second blue-winged olive hatch of the season begins in September. They hatch mornings and afternoons. Use the Parawulff BWO #16 on top and trail with Barr's BWO Emerger #18 to #20. I've seen pale morning duns still sticking around into September, and the fish do take them on top.

I particularly like August and September because the wading is easier—flows are down to 200 to 300 c.f.s., and the low water tends to concentrate fish in smaller areas. It also requires a little more stealth, since the fish can see you more easily.

8. Big Thompson River below Estes Park

The section of the Big Thompson River discussed in this book begins below Lake Estes in Estes Park and winds 20 miles down a canyon into the city of Loveland. If you are traveling from Denver, Loveland is about 50 miles north on US 287 or I-25. From Loveland take US 34 to the mouth of the canyon.

In 1976 a flood destroyed much of the canyon, which resulted in a major habitat restoration effort and created one of the most popular and productive trout fisheries on the Front Range. Along with the nearby Poudre River, the Big Thompson was selected as the site of the 2006 National Fly Fishing Championship. The only meadow stream habitat is a half-mile stretch beneath the dam on Lake Estes. The remainder is composed of rapids, riffles, runs, and pools.

Population
Even though whirling disease organisms are present, the Big Thompson is one of only two rivers in the state to have a healthy reproducing rainbow trout population. A trout population survey in a 572-foot section of the Big Thompson below Olympus Dam in 2009 estimated there were 149 rainbows and 112 brown trout larger than 6 inches, with the most common sizes being 12 to 14 inches. Some fish were as large as 16 inches. A 24-inch brown was captured in 2009 during a fish survey, close to a popular picnic ground in the lower river.

Flows
With an average high flow of 250 cubic feet per second coming in early June (dropping off quickly to 125 to 150 c.f.s. for the rest of the summer), the Big Thompson is one of the most fishable rivers in the state for 10 months of the year.

Access
Parking is at a premium, so plan to do some hiking along the road. The stretch from the Estes dam to Waltonia Bridge is catch-and-release, flies and lures only. Regular regulations are in force from Waltonia Bridge to the city of Loveland, which means the fishing generally drops off in this stretch.

An angler explores the Big Thompson River in Forrest Canyon of Rocky Mountain National Park. TIM ROMANO

Summer Strategy

The relatively short period of runoff simplifies the decision making on the Big Thompson. And so does the hatch timing because, like the nearby Cache La Poudre, the angler will find midges, green drakes, red quills, caddis, and stoneflies all active during the months of July and August. It's important to have a selection of dry flies, because if the bugs are hatching, the fish will lock in on the hatch. If nothing is coming off the water, a good selection of nymphs, larvae, and emergers in those insects is necessary.

Tactics and Flies

The hatches are sporadic if it's sunny, but all of the above insects will hatch in the afternoon. The red quill mayflies, the green drakes, and the big stoneflies will be on the move in the morning as well. An overcast day will probably increase the hatches.

The caddis hatch begins during runoff in June and lasts until September. For dry flies use the Clown Shoe Caddis green or brown, #14 to #16, or the old standby, Elkhair Caddis #12 to #18 in tan, brown, or green.

The green drakes will hatch in July and August. For adult drakes try Lawson's Parachute Green Drake #10 to #12. For nymphs use the Crown Jewel Green Drake nymph #10 to #12. Trail a Mercury or Black Beauty midge larva #18 to #20 beneath either the dry or nymph. The golden stoneflies hatch from early June into September. Try K's Golden Stone #8 to #12. The red quill mayflies, which hatch July to August, are more likely to be hot pink than red. A.K.'s Melon Quill #14 to #16 is a killer for this hatch, or go with a Pheasant Tail Nymph #14 to #18 when there is no obvious hatch.

> ## PRO TIP
>
> About 2 miles up the canyon, there is a water diversion and parking area on the south side of the highway. The stretch of river from there to where the river crosses under the road (about ¼ mile) is excellent fishing, with rainbows and browns up to 14 inches. Riprap along the elevated highway makes hiking along the river difficult, but it's worth it. When the runoff has lowered, it is also possible (albeit tricky) to wade.
>
> The Big Thompson River above Estes Park is also worth a trip for brook trout and cutthroats.

NORTHWEST REGION

9. TRAPPERS LAKE

One of the most beautiful, accessible, angler-friendly lakes in Colorado, Trappers Lake is a natural, 200-acre, 180-foot-deep jewel nestled among dense fir, pine, and spruce forest at 9,600 feet in the Flat Tops Wilderness. Immense lava walls tower 1,500 feet above the lake's eastern edge. From Denver take I-70 west for 190 miles to the city of Rifle, then CO 13 north for 42 miles through the town of Meeker. Stay on Rio Blanco CR 8 for 39 miles and east on Trappers Lake Road for 11 miles. There are three parking lots at the end of the road.

Population

This lake is populated with Colorado River cutthroat trout and to a lesser degree with brook trout. The cutthroats average 12 to 14 inches, with some as large as 18 inches. The brookies tend to be smaller.

Access

About half the lakeshore is walkable, but less than that is wadable because the lake drops off very quickly in some areas. It is open to nonmotorized fishing craft, and some boats are available for renting. When the lake level drops after mid-July, more of the lake becomes wadable. It gets pretty windy on the lake, so a stout rod is necessary. There are very affordable campgrounds on the east side of the lake, and reservations are not required. Since it's about 40 miles to the nearest town, camping is a good way to hit the best fishing times. It's a popular spot but not overrun, and midweek is the best time to show up. For most of the summer, mosquitoes are fierce. The whole of the Flat Tops Wilderness (which literally surrounds Trappers Lake) is like a giant high-altitude swamp. Bring protective mosquito gear or douse yourself with repellent, or you won't have a very good time.

> ### PRO TIP
>
> The best fishing is just after ice-out in the middle of June. Coincidentally (but just as importantly), the mosquitoes haven't yet gotten too bad.

The author caught a 14-inch cutthroat after wrist-stripping an emerger in Trappers Lake. The ice melts late in this high-altitude, natural lake. MICHAEL JONES

Summer Strategy

The strategy for Trappers Lake hinges on the aquatic plants that grow around the lake, from the shoreline to a maximum depth of 15 to 20 feet. That's where most of the insects hatch and where the fish will congregate, either holding over the plants or cruising above them. They ring the entire lake to one degree or another. It's the perfect place for a float tube, since some of the bank is difficult to walk. Don't be tempted to rent a canoe unless you're already used to fly fishing from one; canoes make casting awkward and are prone to giving anglers a sore back.

For wading, the northeast corner of the lake (from the parking lot) is excellent because the lake bed slopes gently out for 20 to 30 feet and drops off steeply. Many fish congregate at the drop-off point. If you rent a boat, fish the drop-offs from out in the lake facing the shore. When the wind blows, and if there is a hatch on, the trout will congregate in glassy water on the leeward side of the lake and feed on top. Midges are a staple for trout on the lake and will hatch anytime the water is calm. The only significant mayfly hatch is the *Callibaetis*. In August *Callibaetis* duns hatch prodigiously just beyond the drop-off areas in the evenings. They return to lay their eggs late the next morning. In nature the *Callibaetis* vary in color from gray to creamy to olive. In Trappers Lake they tend to be more olive.

A mild wind that raises choppy water can still hold fish at fairly shallow depths, so if you can position yourself with the wind at your back, the fishing can still be great. Algae takes over much of the lake beginning in early August.

Tactics and Flies

As with most Colorado fly fishing, a 9-foot 5W rod works best—medium flexibility for dry flies, a little stiffer for weighted nymphs, streamers, and windy conditions. The *Callibaetis* hatch begins in late June and extends into September. During late mornings, early afternoons, or overcast days, clouds of insects appear over the water, and fish eat voraciously. At these times a simple Adams or Blue Dun #14 to #16 will take fish, or almost any attractor dry fly will do. If you fish emergers or nymphs, try regular Pheasant Tails or olive Gold Ribbed Hare's Ear Nymphs in #14 to #16, and strip these quickly, 24 to 30 inches at a time. According to Al Marlowe (a local angler who's fished Trappers Lake too many times to count and written his own book about it), these flies and method will often work when nothing else does.

Caddis, too, occur about the same time as *Callibaetis*, but the hatches never are as thick as the *Callibaetis* hatches. In these between times, fish an Elkhair Caddis dry, #16 to #18. Scuds, which are crustaceans like shrimp, are a major food source for Trappers Lake cutthroats. Throw a slightly weighted scud imitation to the edge of weed beds, and use the hand roll retrieval (3 to 4 inches at a time), letting it sink for a few seconds between retrievals.

It's good to know all the above but truthfully, just experiment with standard attractor dry flies and emergers. Trout circle the lake above the weed beds and will often hit anything that's close to a bug and moving. I've had good fishing at Trappers using little more than a wrist roll retrieve with a gray Krystal RS-2 Emerger #16 to #18.

10. Flat Tops Wilderness Lakes

This wilderness compares to few others in the West. Approximately 110 trout-laden lakes and ponds, often unnamed, dot the country below flattopped cliffs. With about 50 miles of streams crisscrossing the wilderness serving as other habitats for trout, this place is an angler's paradise. It comprises 235,000 acres of land between the altitudes of 7,500 feet and 13,000 feet.

With access from Trappers Lake, decent fishing is possible in most of the lakes except for the highest altitude, shallowest lakes in the Flat Tops. I've picked three of the best spots within reasonable access from Trappers Lake to feature. There are two other accesses into the Flat Tops—the Deep Creek access (as named by locals), otherwise known as Forest Road 600, and the Sweetwater Creek access, both of which access the east side of the wilderness. To reach these places turn north on the Colorado River Road off I-70 at Dotsero, between Eagle and Glenwood Springs. The Sweetwater Creek access is about 2 miles up the CRR, and Sweetwater Creek is about 10 miles up that road from the turnoff. Deep Creek Road is 4WD, high-access vehicles only. Sweetwater Creek Road is a well-maintained gravel county road to the wilderness boundary. I'm familiar with the wilderness because I worked on a ranch in Sweetwater Creek canyon for two summers while I was in college.

Population
While there are reportedly a lot of fish, no formal surveys have been done.

Access
Coffin Lake is just a 30-minute hike from the parking area on the north side of Trappers Lake. Follow Trail 1814 for 4 miles along the north, then the east side of Trappers Lake to 6-acre Coffin Lake.

Little Trappers Lake is another mile or so farther, and it's quite a bit smaller than Trappers Lake.

Wall Lake (45 acres, at almost 11,000 feet) is also accessed from Trappers Lake by hiking south on Trail 1818 for approximately 6 miles. The hike is rated as strenuous.

The Flat Top Wilderness is, as I mentioned above, a lush, verdant place filled with potholes of water and streams. There are quite a few unmarked trails, used by horses as well as hikers. Except in unusually dry years, these trails are often muddy. And with the exception of Coffin Lake, hiking to these lakes requires planning for an all-day outing. Prepare for inclement weather, with good hiking boots, rain gear, and food and water, or better yet an overnight to take advantage of evening and morning hatches in warm weather.

Be prepared for mosquitoes and rain, some time away from camp, and a strenuous hike. An altitude gain of 1,000 feet over 1 mile, especially at that altitude, is no picnic.

Summer Strategy

Virtually the same as for Trappers Lake, the strategy for Flat Tops Wilderness Lakes revolves around the aquatic plants that grow around the lake from the shoreline to a maximum depth of 15 to 20 feet. As most insects hatch there, the fish will hold over the plants or cruise above them. It's a perfect site for a float tube; I don't recommend using canoes here.

These lakes are considerably smaller than Trappers, so the natural dynamics are less robust. These smaller lakes freeze longer and deeper, and while they may have many of the same insect species, the fish will generally be smaller in size, fewer in number, and hungrier and more willing to bite anything that remotely looks like food. They will be more active in overcast, cool weather and in early mornings or evenings, when the bugs are active.

Tactics and Flies

These lakes all require a similar fishing methodology. Survey the water, and find those places where wading is possible and where the brush and trees along the shore will allow for backcasting. If you're fishing wet flies, you can also roll cast, or you can wade out and backcast over the water and drop flies close in to the bank. Fish also tend to congregate near outlets and inlets because the food supply is more condensed there.

The feeding season is so short in these high lakes that the fish often have to eat a lot in a short time to survive the winters. There are 20-inch-long cutthroat trout in Coffin and Wall Lakes. Try fishing Hare's Ear Nymphs, Adams and Griffin's Gnat dry flies, Prince Nymphs, scuds, mosquito patterns, Pheasant Tail Nymphs, caddis dry flies and larvae, ants, beetles, and midge patterns. Throw in some attractor dry flies, such as the Royal Wulff, red or yellow Humpy, Rio Grande Trude, and Rio Grande King, and if things get slow try a black leech against the bottom just inside the weed beds, retrieved with slow, mildly jerky movements.

11. Blue River

Beginning as a trickle at high altitude, the Blue is a small mountain stream until it reaches the valley above Breckenridge, at which time it becomes a more meandering, slower water with a number of trout habitat improvements before it reaches Dillon Reservoir. Immediately below the reservoir the tailwater holds some very large, very wily rainbow trout, some as big as 10 pounds, and quite a few less picky fish in the 13- to 16-inch range. Eight lanes of I-70 coming down from two very long, steep hills roar over the tailwater, leaving an odor of overheated brakes. Many habitat improvements have been built in the first 2 miles, and the channel is relatively wide, which also makes much of the tailwater wadable except during peak runoff. The 15-mile stretch from the tailwater to Green Mountain Reservoir is a classic mountain valley stream, with riffle/run/pool complexes throughout and many large and very large boulders in the water.

If ever there were a fishery that could be a phoenix—risen from the ashes—it would be the Blue. From its headwaters down to the town of Breckenridge, the stream historically ran through mining operations, which poisoned the water with heavy metals. More recently, in the river downstream from the dam on Dillon Reservoir, whirling disease wiped out rainbow trout for 20 years, although, inexplicably, most tailwaters of WD-positive rivers have maintained a healthy rainbow population throughout the years in waters immediately below their dams. A number of hazardous chemical spills over the past decade and 6 years of drought have wiped out generations of brown trout.

But today, from top to bottom, this is a beautiful, healthy, productive trout river, due in large part to reclamation of mine sites, habitat improvements, and restrictions to protect trout populations. It is now possible to have a fairly extraordinary experience in urban fishing, at least in the tailwater section, where you can walk from the ol' fishin' hole to a cold beer or a latte, a Big Gulp or a microwave burrito. Maybe even pick up a pair of Levis or Nike running shoes at discount prices. Waders are generally frowned on in such establishments, however, unless you flash a Titanium Am/Ex card. Then all is forgiven.

Population

The Blue River from the Dillon dam downstream to Green Mountain Reservoir is rated as a Gold Medal Water, meaning the area has a high

An angler looks for just the right fly to match the hatch. TIM ROMANO

potential for trophy trout. All are fly and lure only, with immediate release of the fish. No fish survey results are available from the Colorado Division of Wildlife, but the DOW began stocking whirling disease–resistant Hofer strains of rainbows in 2009, so fishing success on the river below Dillon Reservoir should be on the rise.

Flows

The yearly average flow on the Blue River below the reservoir is about 125 cubic feet per second. Beginning in late May dam releases increase the water level very quickly to as high as 2,000 c.f.s., and it falls just as rapidly by July to normal. Once runoff starts just stay out of the water: 500 c.f.s. on this stretch of river is too much for safety or success.

Access

There is excellent access on the river above Dillon Reservoir, by the tail-water section, and downstream to Green Mountain Reservoir and below. The access points are usually near habitat improvements or generally fine stretches of fishing water. The first access is the Blue River Campground, which is 6 miles from Silverthorne. Sutton Unit State Wildlife Area is 7 miles from town, Eagle's Nest Wildlife Area is 9 miles, and the Blue River Wildlife Area 17 miles. Most of the river above Dillon Reservoir and adjacent to Breckenridge is along the highway and has a bike/pedestrian path. The areas that are private are clearly marked.

Summer Strategy

This is a perfect fishery for all levels of ability. The river above Dillon Reservoir is great for beginners and children. The only problem is that run-off swells the river for a longer period than it does below the reservoir, raising the water to high levels for a couple of months. Before and after runoff, access is easy and comfortable. Much of the river is right in the town limits of Breckenridge and has habitat improvements. The tailwater stretch, at least the first mile or so, requires anglers of an expert technical level to have much chance of catching fish. The successful anglers fish this stretch regularly, can sight-fish to specific fish, and create a natural presentation over and over again. Anything that looks suspicious, including shiny split shot or beads, drifts that are too fast or too slow, or line flash and splash, will put a fish down. But get it right, and wow, you have a show that will have shoppers on the path or on the pedestrian bridges over the river applauding and demanding encores.

Fortunately for the rest of us, the Blue River below the tailwater is just a great fishery, and normal techniques and presentations will catch fish, unless the cranky fish simply decide not to eat. Which happens sometimes.

With a full offering of rainbows, cuttbows, browns, and Kokanee salmon (in November), what more could you ask for from this fishery?

Tactics and Flies

For the summer season (from after the peak of runoff to the end of September), golden stoneflies are the first insects of note to hatch on the Blue, beginning in early June and lasting until the end of July. Considering that runoff is often unfishable until July, the angler should fish nymphs in both the morning and the afternoon, when the stones start landing on the water. The second phase of golden stones' evolution takes place on above-water rocks and bankside brush, so emergers are not a factor. For nymphs try any golden stone pattern, such as K's Golden Stones #6 to #10 or any number of epoxy-backed stone patterns. In high water look for slow spots along the bank and pocket water—behind or in front of boulders—any place with a slower current and a hydraulic buffer where the fish can rest. When the water slows down and smooth water pockets emerge, cast a yellow Stimulator #8 to #12. When the flat water returns to the tailwater, try a mysis shrimp pattern #16 to #18 or use tandem mayfly and/or midge nymphs #16 to #22 or some combination of the above three choices with a white strike indicator and green split shot. If nothing else is working, try a peach egg tandem with an IED #12, which is a red, beaded San Juan Worm.

Caddis hatches occur in the afternoons and evenings from June to September. A tandem rig using a dry fly such as the Clown Shoe Caddis #14 to #18 and an emerger such as a Sparkle Caddis #16 to #18 is recommended.

PRO TIP

According to Cutthroat Anglers in Silverthorne, keep an eye on the reservoir level. In high snowpack years the water will spill over the dam, adding warmer water to the river and inciting increased insect hatch and trout feeding activity. If you are fishing during high flows, they also suggest staying close to the bank and fishing smooth water, instead of wading into the smooth waters and fishing to fast currents. The trout like the smooth waters, too.

When the water is still too high to see fish or even subsurface structure, pick a 20-by-20-foot section of water, and cast methodically using the high stick drift (raising the rod so the fly line above the indicator or dry fly is out of the water) from close in to farther out so you don't spook a fish with the line. If there's no interest from below, move upstream, and try a different fly selection.

By early July the green drake mayflies will begin hatching. Whenever the drakes are around, use a dry, something like a Parachute Adams #10 to #12, with an emerger or a nymph dropper #10 to #12, unweighted so it stays close to the surface (drakes emerge from the nymphal shucks just below the surface). Or just use a dry fly pattern such as a Parachute Green Drake #10 to #12, and be ready for the action. Fish will key on drakes whenever they're on the water.

Yellow Sally stoneflies and pale morning dun mayflies both hatch in July, and the PMDs will continue into September. But in July sometimes one dry fly pattern such as the Comparadun PMD #16 will work for both.

When the summer doldrums hit in August (usually late in August and early September), try attractor dry fly patterns such as a yellow or red Humpy, a Royal Wulff, or a beetle and hopper pattern #14 to #16.

12. WILLIAMS FORK RIVER BELOW WILLIAMS FORK RESERVOIR

The Williams Fork River tailwater is a 2-mile section between Williams Fork Reservoir and a confluence with the Colorado River. The confluence occurs near the town of Parshall on US 40, between the towns of Hot Sulphur Springs and Kremmling. The river features riffles, runs, and deep pools with undercut banks in narrow spots.

Since the Williams Fork River in this section is bookended by a reservoir and the Colorado River, it's populated with fish from both ends. In fact, flushing flows from the reservoir in 1996 and 1998 dumped thousands of brown trout and (some) rainbows into the tailwater and the Colorado River. While rainbow reproduction was mostly wiped out by whirling disease in the 1990s, and brown trout populations have been on the decline, many of those remaining fish prefer, for a variety of reasons, to spend time in the Williams Fork tailwater.

Population

While the number of brown trout have generally declined in the Colorado River, angler reports have consistently reported good fishing on the Williams Fork tailwater. The average size of fish caught has been about 14 inches. Rainbow trout represent less than 1 percent of fish sampled or caught.

Flows

The yearly average flow, minus the month of June, is about 100 cubic feet per second. During June 2010 runoff/dam releases hit 2,000 c.f.s., but the snowpack in central Colorado was well above average that year. More normal runoff reaches 1,000 to 1,500 c.f.s. The Williams Fork river channel is not particularly wide, so 500 c.f.s. pretty much makes the river unfishable from mid-May to early July. There are periodic low flows of 20 to 50 c.f.s, which stress the trout badly, particularly during spawning seasons, and fishing at those times is generally discouraged.

> **PRO TIP**
>
> Take plenty of mosquito repellent. There are a lot of irrigated hay fields in the vicinity, and the mosquitoes are numerous and ornery.

Access

To reach the river turn south at Parshall on CR 3 for 1 mile to a parking area, then hike about 1 mile. When the Colorado River is wadable, go to the first access west of Parshall, cross the river, and walk east to the confluence of the Williams Fork and Colorado Rivers, then work upstream.

Summer Strategy

Fishing the Williams Fork from the end of runoff to the end of September is fairly simple. If there's no obvious hatch on, fish attractor dry flies, emergers, and nymphs. If a hatch comes off, match the hatch. For some reason the deep pools on the Williams Fork seem less productive than fishing the riffles, edges of runs, and pocket water. Most everybody agrees on this, and it makes little sense unless anglers are not getting flies to the correct depth in the pools. They are deep and not always clear. Sure enough, every time I've fished the Williams Fork, I've started with the pools but had little success until I moved into faster water.

Tactics and Flies

There are six major hatches from early July to September, including three mayfly hatches—pale morning duns, green drakes, and red quills—with tricos beginning in early August and lasting well into October in the mornings. At the same time large golden stoneflies, caddis, and small yellow Sallies will be hatching, with the caddis hatching well into September. Given the number of mayflies present, expect good hatches if the weather is cloudy, with PMDs in the morning and evenings and the other species in afternoon to evening hatches. Blue-winged olives will be hatching beginning in mid-September. If there is one hatch that stirs the kind of excitement anglers dream about, it's the BWO hatches in spring and late summer/early fall. A 6X tippet might be needed at times if the hatching insects are smaller than normal, which isn't unusual because of the relatively low water temperature.

While dry fly fishing isn't a huge factor on this short stretch of water, most anglers use a dry/dropper setup for the runs and riffles or an emerger/nymph setup with plenty of weight for the deep pools. The split shot should be bouncing on the bottom from time to time if you have the proper weight and strike indicator position. The split shot should be a minimum 18 inches above the first fly. Don't be afraid to make adjustments.

If the summer doldrums seem to have set in, try a Parachute Hopper #12 to #16 or a Kiwi Beetle #12 to #14, and plop it on the water.

For caddis dry flies a simple tan, olive, or brown Elkhair Caddis or Hi-Vis Clownshoe Caddis #14 to #18 is hard to beat. For the bottom fly on dry/dropper, a Buckskin #14 to #18 or a green or tan Caddis Larvae #14 to #18 are generally effective. For PMDs and the rusty spinners use a Sparkle Dun #14 to #18 and a Pheasant Tail Nymph #16 to #18.

SOUTHEAST REGION

13. ARKANSAS RIVER

The Arkansas River is born along the slopes of Colorado's Collegiate Peaks, southwest of Leadville. There are 150 miles of free-flowing brown trout water before it pours into the plains east of the city of Pueblo. Almost all is open to floating, but only about 75 miles is open to foot access—more than enough for a lifetime of fishing.

Powerful, beautiful, raging, fecund, intimidating—the size and diversity of the Arkansas make it difficult to fish, but more and more people are coming to it precisely because of its diversity (as well as its generous public access). But it's sometimes still possible, except during the misnamed Mother's Day caddis hatch (which actually begins in the lower reaches about April 15), to fish some of the river with a feeling of solitude. The state park's boat launch sites and picnic grounds, however, are often crowded.

Population

A river the size of the Arkansas is very difficult to do a fish population census on, but some suggest there are many stretches with incredible numbers of brown trout. One thing everybody agrees upon is that it's a river on its way up. Since 1993 mine tailings that had been polluting the river and stunting the growth of fish have been largely curtailed. One local outfitter/guide—Bill Edrington of Royal Gorge Anglers in Cañon City—has estimated there are as many as 4,000 brown trout per mile in many stretches of the river between the towns of Salida and Cañon City, estimates based upon periodic Division of Wildlife surveys, as well as the number of fish that rise to the surface during the blanket caddis hatches. Above Salida there are still plenty of fish, but possibly not as many because of the fast current in the canyons.

Flows

Water releases from numerous impoundments on feeder streams, as well as seasonal runoff, make much of the river unfishable from mid-May to early July, with the peak flows reaching 3,000 to 4,000 cubic feet per second. These flows also attract many thousands of rafters to the Arkansas, which by consensus is one of the, if not the, most heavily rafted rivers in the country: all the more reason to avoid it for walk-in/wade fishing during this time. As the water levels drop, so do the number of rafters.

Access

The Arkansas is managed by a consortium of local, state, and federal agencies called the Arkansas Headwaters Recreation Association. This group has produced a detailed and accurate map of the river and public access areas. It is given away locally along the river and by the Arkansas Headwaters Recreation Area at 307 W. Sackett, Salida, CO 81201.

Summer Strategy

It's difficult to be a fishing expert about a 150-mile stretch of river, so I have used Bill Edrington and his book, *Fly Fishing the Arkansas,* as my resource. He's fished the Arkansas for 30 years, 20 as a guide and educator about all things trout. For anyone interested in understanding the river, his book is a must. It's available locally and from RoyalGorgeAnglers.com.

For strategic, trout-fishing purposes, the Arkansas River can be divided into five sections. The first access, moving from upstream to down, is the Hayden Ranch, beginning at the US 24 bridge across the river about 8 miles south of Leadville, extending 5 miles downstream to the Granite access. The next is from Granite down to Buena Vista. The third is from Buena Vista to Salida, the fourth from Salida to Cañon City, and, finally, below Pueblo Reservoir through the city of Pueblo.

The 5-mile stretch of the Hayden Ranch is entirely accessible. There are two parking areas, one at the north end and another about 3 miles south, opening the lower section to upstream and downstream access. I prefer the lower access (Kobe access) because the riparian zone isn't as heavily grazed as the upper and the river exhibits more holding water, such as undercut banks, pools, and riffles. While dozens of streams dump water into the lower reaches of the Arkansas, only a couple do so in this stretch, so it is the first to become wadable. It is also a meandering meadow stream in this stretch. Unfortunately, it can also be the coldest. In the early summer season, this is streamer water. The section from the bottom of Hayden Ranch down to Balltown (just above the Twin Lakes Reservoir outlet) is physically more varied and includes riffles, runs, and pools but is still wadable.

By July the water is down quite a bit, is only slightly off color, and features one of the only green drake hatches on the river. By August it's nearly

Jessie Wyard holds a nice summer brown trout caught on the Arkansas.
RUSSELL MILLER

clear and usually wadable. The stretch from Balltown to Buena Vista squeezes water into a canyon with some public access, but it also picks up the overflow from Twin Lakes Reservoir. It's usually high and fast until mid-August. I've looked at the river at these times but decided not to fish it because of these conditions. Edrington says, however, that this stretch is worth fishing, and I will defer to his judgment.

The river below Buena Vista down to Salida begins in a canyon. The Browns Canyon stretch is one of the wildest, hairiest pieces of water anywhere and one of the most popular technical rafting and kayaking destinations in the state. Besides Browns Canyon, the river is wide and meandering, with manageable banks in most places. The water is beautiful and looks wadable but is deceptively swift, even at calf-high levels, so tread carefully, use a wading staff, a wading belt, and spike-soled felt or rubber boots.

The water stays high in this stretch until mid- to late August, when the reservoirs stop dumping irrigation flows. But even in swifter water, as long as the banks are negotiable, anglers fish along the banks, where the flow velocity is lower. The fish stack there, darting into fast water for tasty morsels. In many places wading isn't necessary because the current is such that an angler is difficult to see unless he or she is throwing a shadow on the water.

From Salida downstream to Cañon City, things get interesting. The highway follows the river, and at least one bank is accessible most of the way. Parking lots and restroom facilities, boat ramps, and picnic areas are available. The area directly downstream from Salida to Rincon is rated Gold Medal and is 75 percent open to the public on at least one bank. Downstream to Cotopaxie are the Treat/Ogden fishing leases, Vallie Bridge boat launch site. Downstream from Cotopaxie to Parkdale are the Loma Linda area, Lone Pine Recreation Area, Pinnacle Rock access, Five Points, Spike Buck, and Parkdale developed accesses, with some amenities.

The Royal Gorge is not recommended for fishing (there are safety concerns, and the fishing is generally poor) but there are about 4 miles of great access and fishing after the river exits the gorge. On 3 miles of those there's a lovely recreation area with benches, outhouses, and a well-maintained trail. Below Cañon City there is no river fishing until below the dam at Pueblo Reservoir, which isn't worth much in the summer because of high flows. But it has become one of the most popular areas for winter fishing because of the banana-belt effect (consistently about 10 degrees warmer than Denver), some excellent habitat improvements, and regular stocking of rainbow trout.

Since I count the "summer season" as being from peak of runoff to the end of September, the angler is really looking at the months of July, August, and September. A more realistic approach would be to wait until mid-August for the best chance of a successful outing. Although the Arkansas can be successfully fished in high water using certain tactics, the best fishing will be in the late spring and early fall. I can testify to the fact that driving along looking at the river it's difficult not to stop and toss a line.

Tactics and Flies

Because of the variable conditions, this is a water that cries out for a 2-fly setup: hopper/dropper (nymph or emerger), emerger/nymph, 2 nymphs, 2 dry flies, dry fly, and nymph. A 9-foot 5W rod will cover most situations on this river, although if you are planning on throwing some heavy nymphs, a longer, heavier rod is preferable.

When the water is high, as it will be in early summer, remember that the fast water will drive fish in toward the shore. They will literally be stacked like firewood along the banks, often at 2 to 3 feet of depth.

The first insect hatch of note—golden stoneflies—will hit its peak about the same time the high water level peaks. Try a K's Golden Stonefly Nymph #8 to #12 on top and a green or cream caddis pattern, such as Barr's Net Builder Caddis #14 to #16 or a Buckskin Caddis #14 to #18. Cast up and across cast into the side current using a high-stick drift and an indicator that puts the top fly close to the bottom. Lower the tip as the line goes past, and raise the tip again as the line swings across the current and becomes parallel to the bank. This both simulates an emerging caddis and puts you in position for a water-to-water cast, which is critical if you are casting from the bank or shallow water against the bank.

Another golden opportunity is in late June and early July when the water is high but clear and fish huddle next to rock outcroppings and cut banks. The golden stones are hatching, along with PMDs. Hopper/dropper rigs rule.

As the water level drops, this combo will work for the remainder of the summer and is always worth a try. The lower and warmer the water gets, you'll have to work the riffles instead of flat water, because the fish will hold in the highly oxygenated water of the riffles looking for stonefly nymphs. If you can't resist throwing a few dry flies, just plop a yellow or orange Stimulator #10 to #12 in slow water and try for a short, natural drift. It won't take long to see if the fish are interested.

The second major hatch of summer season is the green drake. That hatch starts about July 1 and works its way upriver from Buena Vista to the Hayden Ranch access. It does not occur below Buena Vista to any significant extent. The areas above Buena Vista are often considered unfishable earlier in the summer. The Hayden Ranch access usually becomes manageable by July 1, depending upon snowpack. The drakes will hang about all summer to

PRO TIP

If all else fails, tie on an orange Stimulator and drop a bead head Prince Nymph, both in #10. If fished correctly, Bill Edrington says it'll take fish 365 days a year.

some extent. A Parachute Green Drake or a Parachute or regular Adams #10 to #12 will draw these fish to the top.

Bill Edrington points out that there are at least 75 species of caddis on the Arkansas, but many of those would be difficult for the angler to identify. Exactly matching any type of caddis coming off the water (there could be 5 to 7 species at any given time) could be a waste of energy for the newcomer.

Active hatch or not, caddis will launch quickly from oxygenated riffle water in the morning and return to slack water to drop their eggs. If they do hatch in the afternoons, they will return to lay eggs the following morning. You could probably use a dry fly such as an Elkhair Caddis at either time and maybe catch a fish, but you increase your odds considerably by using a hopper pattern on top and an emerger pattern such as the Bracy Pupa #16, dropped 18 to 24 inches off the hopper's hook, or better yet, use a golden stonefly nymph such as Larry Kingery's Arkansas Rubber Leg Stone #4 to #10 on top and a bead head Caddis Pupa #16 as the dropper in a double-nymph rig. The point is to get the browns to hit the emerger at the end of the drift when it's rising up through the water column. And it's pretty exciting: The fish hit aggressively because the emergers launch like little rocket ships when they're rising. You want the end of the drift to rise in fast water, just like the real bugs.

For the egg-laying side of the equation, the most effective rig would be an egg-layer pattern on top and a spent caddis dropped off 18 to 24 inches. These rigs should be cast into slow water along the river's banks or behind large rocks, submerged or not. These should be fished as dry flies. The foam patterns have been very effective in recent years.

An egg-layer caddis will have either an extended body, as if it's dragging its egg sack and guts, or a "hot butt," which is another color from the body—typically red, green, or yellow. In the case of spent caddis, the wings will be splayed to each side perpendicular to or somewhat in the water beside the body. In recent years I've used a Hornberg #12 to #16, which is technically a streamer but floats very well naturally until it absorbs water, and I've caught a number of decent-size fish on the surface. Once it gets wet I've caught fish dead-drifting it, on the downstream swing as an emerger, or even just letting it float straight downstream and letting it swing back and forth in the current—but not stripping it as streamers are usually fished, for some mysterious reason. I think it must resemble a spent caddis when floating because the bottom half of the wing is immediately submerged when it hits the water.

Rafters on the Arkansas take a break from the river. Tim Romano

If you just have to try to match the hatch and fish dries, you'd better have a good selection of sizes and colors. Start by searching the bushes along the banks to see which caddis are more numerous, and pick a fly that most resembles the insect.

In fact, Edrington says that the Arkansas River brown trout will just as likely take attractor flies as anything more visually accurate, flies like the Yellow Humpy, Royal Wulff, Renegade, and Royal Coachman Trude on top and nymphs like Pheasant Tails, Hare's Ears, and Prince Nymphs as the dropper flies.

Once the river comes down in August and September, terrestrial insects such as the grasshopper and beetles—especially the hopper—become a major food source for the fish. While many use outlandish hopper designs for the hopper/dropper rigs, I think more realistic designs are more effective when the hoppers are flying around. Drop a black foam beetle behind the natural hopper pattern, and you've got a double whammy. Hoppers are good for pulling lethargic fish off the bottom because they're such a large meal.

In September keep your eyes open for the smallish, gray blue-winged olive mayflies, because later in the season these will become the primary food source going into winter. There should be more and more of these as the water cools and especially in overcast weather, which we don't get a lot of during the summer. The hatches are early in the day, and the BWOs lay their eggs in the evenings when the weather is hot, but both should move more toward the middle of the day as the water cools. With quite a bit of flat water around, this is prime dry fly time. Put a standard Parachute Adams or a Parawulff BWO, both in sizes #16 to #20, as your top fly and a bead head Pheasant Tail Nymph #16 to #20 or an olive bead head Hare's Ear #16 to #20 as your dropper. I highly recommend using an emerger pattern such as Barr's BWO Emerger #14 to #20 as a dropper or an emerger as the top fly and a nymph as the bottom, weighted enough to get down into pools but not necessarily on the bottom, as these tiny flies will get caught in the current and can be at any depth.

SUMMER SEASON SUMMARY

If you ever needed evidence that the Great Spirit has a sense of humor, just think about the irony of having high runoff coincide with some of the better hatches and best weather of the season. Then he turns around and gives us green drake hatches after the flows have settled. If you have the opportunity, go after the green drakes on the Lake Fork of the Gunnison, the Big Thompson River, or the Blue River downstream from the tailwater. These will all begin hatching in June, on through July, and even into August and occasionally into September. The best ones are early. So it would be smart to leave a few days open and stay in communication with a local fly shop of your choice. Take advantage of fishes' basic energy-saving strategy, and use green drake cripples and spinners, or run a 2-nymph rig with a green drake on top and a golden stone on the bottom.

FALL

OCTOBER, NOVEMBER, AND DECEMBER

In most ways autumn is my favorite time to fish. It's usually the best weather of the year, the mosquitoes are history, the aspens are turning, and the water is usually low enough to wade easily. It's often clear enough to see the fish in the water, and the fish have become opportunistic feeders as they try to fatten up for the winter. And the daytime fishing moves more to the middle of the day as the water cools and the fish become more active. Also, there are fewer anglers to deal with, maybe because they've used all their vacation time fishing in August and September.

Besides taking streamers for food, the browns become downright cantankerous about the presence of fish or streamers near their spawning beds and attack the interlopers. There's not much more fun in fly fishing than feeling these aggressive strikes.

In conjunction with the brown trout spawn, fish eggs become a major food source. If you hit this just right, it becomes almost embarrassingly easy to catch fish, including some of the biggest fish in the river. Three of the rivers listed also have Kokanee salmon runs in the fall, which offer similar opportunities. An advantage to the Kokanee fall run is that these spawning, freshwater salmon die at the end of the run, so anglers can keep some fine-tasting fish without straining their consciences.

Last but certainly not least, the fall consistently contains some of the best dry fly action of the year. Hatches of tiny blue-winged olive mayflies and even tinier midges may rival or exceed the best hatches of the summer, particularly on overcast days (which are more common as the air temperature cools). Depending upon the water flows, an amount of stealth is sometimes required for success. The lower, smoother, and clearer the water is, the more stealth is required. And this means in your approach and casting positions as well as line control and appropriate line sizes.

The fishing conditions and techniques used in the fall, winter, and spring are all relatively similar, with variations made for water and air temperature.

When leaves turn gold in the fall, it's a signal that some of Colorado's best fishing is upon us. For me the best part of autumn fishing is the streamers—and spawning brown trout. Tim Romano

As the water gets colder, the more lethargic fish will tend to hold in slower, deeper water to save energy.

Flies in sizes #12 to #18 should be tied on 5X leaders and tippets. A trailing fly, whether dry or subsurface, is often going to be a size or two smaller as a rule, so that sizes #18 to #22 should be tied on 6X leaders and tippets. Use a monofilament for dries and fluorocarbon for subsurface flies in all 2-fly rigs. For fly sizes #22 to #28, use 7X fluorocarbon. The difference between monofilament nylon and fluorocarbon is that while monofilament is generally stronger and floats slightly better, it also has a higher reflective surface and is a little stiffer. The friction caused by tying knots makes the knots a weaker point in the line. The fluorocarbon sinks a little faster, has a nonreflective surface and a lower friction coefficient, which makes the knots stronger. Moistening the knots with saliva, for either monofilament nylon or fluorocarbon line, is recommended for maximum knot strength.

Fish are spookier in low, clear water because they are more susceptible to predation. Especially during the middle of the day, fish will hold in deeper water or sometimes in the seams between currents. Line splash and flash will put a spooky fish down very quickly, so it's important to fish across the stream and work your way out from near to far. Dress in brown or green to match the background, and if shade is available, use that to mask your presence. Noises in the water such as conspicuous splashes will also tend to spook fish.

Using streamers, you can be somewhat less cautious of the noise your fly makes. A nice plop will alert big fish to the possible presence of prey. Find a channel next to an overhanging bank, then fish from the middle of the river toward the bank. Use the full strip retrieve, 24 to 30 inches, with a couple of seconds' pause between retrieves. If there's a pool, use the same technique.

There are a number of different ways to fish a streamer, each with its adherents. And while the full strip/quick retrieve is the most popular method in the United States, it is not the only method. In New Zealand, for instance, they'll often fish streamers as though they were wet flies—casting across the stream, then dead-drifting with a tight line or high stick. At the end of the dead drift, let the streamer swing back into the current and use a series of lifts or small mends as the line reaches downstream of your position. The lifts and mends will, in theory, make the streamer look alive and thus stimulate a strike.

If you are so inclined, cast upstream, starting from close in to farther out, and begin tightening the line so it's taut when it's directly across. Maintain the tight line throughout the remainder of the drift. This is a good way to fish deeper water, as it allows the weighted streamer to get closer to the bottom. In my experience it's also a good idea to retrieve the fly from downstream by a series of medium or fast strips. I even hang the fly in the current for short periods, letting it sway in the current. (I've even caught fish while wading upstream, dragging a fly in the current—a method I think works better with lightly or unweighted streamers such as a Zonker, Hornberg, or Mickey Finn, mainly because the streamer moves more and stays near the top.)

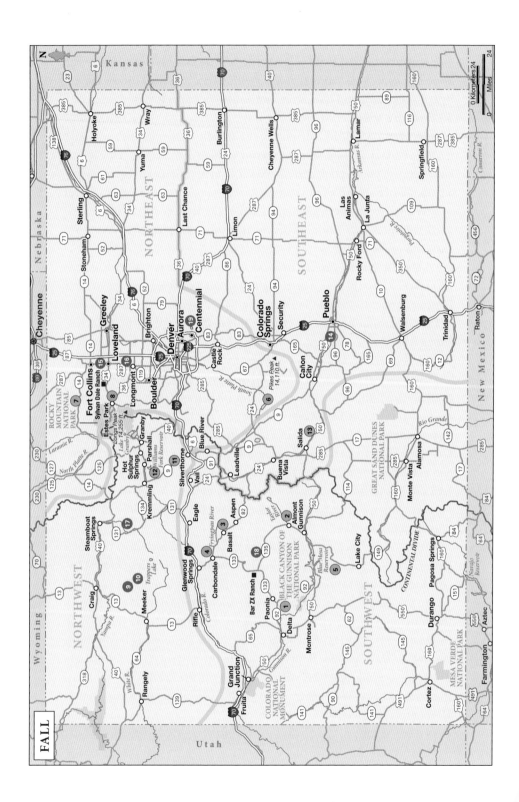

Another tactic worth trying with unweighted streamers is to flick your line from side to side with retrieves that keep the streamer on or near the top of the water. There's nothing a big fish likes more than an easy, big meal represented as a wounded minnow. This fact was driven home to me on the West Fork of the Bitterroot River one summer day when I caught a small brown trout and tried to get it off the hook, which involved much acrobatic splashing. It finally flipped free. Something large bumped my leg; I looked down and saw, for a second or two, a 24-inch bull trout at my feet in 6 inches of water.

Review the summer season section for more information about these fishing sites, and be sure to contact a local fly shop for current, specific information about a particular site. Information is the key to fishing success.

SOUTHWEST REGION

1. Gunnison River in Gunnison Gorge

As mentioned in the summer section, the 14-mile section of the Gunnison River in the Gorge runs between the boundary of the Black Canyon National Park upstream and Pleasure Park downstream, at the confluence with the North Fork of the Gunnison River east of Delta, Colorado, 50 miles south of Grand Junction. It's a true four-season fishery. But for my money fall is perhaps the best time to give it a try, when the brown trout (there's an average of 7,000 per mile) start to spawn and defend their redds.

Population

A 2005 fish census estimated an astounding average of 7,000 brown trout per mile throughout its 14-mile length. Many of those fish are in the 15- to 18-inch range. The largest were 24 to 27 inches long. There was a smattering of rainbows present, but by 2012 the stocking of Hofer whirling disease (WD)–resistant rainbows should bring those numbers up quite a bit.

Flows

The average flow in fall tends to be 400 to 500 cubic feet per second. Flows faster than 500 c.f.s. are considered dangerous.

Access

The four trailheads leading into the upper 7 miles of the gorge can be accessed on Falcon Valley Road from US 50. The junction is a mile south of Olathe and leads to Peach Valley Road, which connects to all four trailheads. These trails are Chukar (1.1 miles long, 500-foot altitude change), Bobcat (1.5 miles, 800 feet), Duncan (1.1 miles, 850 feet), and Ute (4.5 miles, 1,200 feet). But during most of the fall and all winter and spring, just getting to the trailheads by vehicle, because of snow and mud on the near-primitive access roads, is impossible. The trails themselves, often arduous in the summer, are passable in the winter. But conditions should be checked with a local fly shop or the Bureau of Land Management in Montrose.

There are a number of guide services, including Black Canyon Anglers and RIGS Fly Shop, that offer trips in the fall, winter, and spring into the

A beautiful stonefly nymph lazes on a leaf. No wonder the fish love them.
RUSSELL MILLER

upper gorge. If the access roads are impassable, wading anglers are limited to crossing the North Fork of the Gunnison above the confluence with the Gunnison at Pleasure Park and hiking down the 4-mile-long trail on the north side of the Gunnison, up to the Smith Fork River. Pleasure Park is well marked on CO 92, about 12 miles east of Delta. In the fall the North Fork is usually wadable. The bank is extremely manageable on the north side of the river in this area. Even in the lower flows of fall, anglers are encouraged to wear a wading belt, have a wading staff, and wear studded felt or rubber soles. If you hike up to the Smith Fork, which is a feeder stream into the river, you may have the river all to yourself, according to Brian Olson, of Black Canyon Anglers.

Fall Strategy

Fish blue-winged olives early in the season, then a mix of BWOs and midges, then just midges, and use streamers on the ornery, spawning browns. While brown trout predominate in the upper stretch of the river, there are both rainbows and brown trout in the relatively flat water of the stretch between Pleasure Park and the Smith Fork, and they are quite likely some of the biggest fish in the gorge. The fish become more lethargic as the water cools and hold in slack water such as pools and runs.

Tactics and Flies

Because of the width of the river in the lower gorge and the amount of water to be covered, a larger rod might be a good idea. Try a six- or seven-weight, up to 10 feet long, with a leader tapering to 4X thickness. If you're fishing small dries, of course, the leader will have to be tapered with sections of tippets from 5X to 6X or even 7X. A straight 4X leader will be sufficient for streamers.

Unlike in some other tailwaters, strike indicators and split shot or soft weights are advisable in the gorge. Gale Doudy of Gunnison Gorge Anglers, an anglers' association, has developed a system of using both that could be beneficial when nymphing. In fact, I plan to try it the next time I'm on a big water.

First, he says, use an indicator that slows the fly. The speed of the current drops as you go deeper into the water, so a nymph near the bottom moving along at top-water speed is going to look unnatural. A number of poly yarn indicators will take on water without sinking and therefore slow down the rig. (In my opinion the indicator should be green or white rather than pink or red, colors that are less likely to trigger avoidance behavior from the fish.)

It's also important (whether using one fly or two) to have the fly reach the fish prior to the split shot or soft weight. This will have the rig configured in an "L" shape, with the weights at the corner of the intersecting lines of the letter. Experiment with the amount of weight, starting with the lightest and gradually adding split shot as needed at 3-inch intervals, the first about 4 to 6 inches above the top fly. Having multiple weights close together will keep the line below the weights mostly flat instead of in a "V" shape and will help keep the weights from getting caught on the bottom.

This setup works in big water when fishing with tiny flies, situations when the takes can be so subtle that the hook must be set immediately. To see the take an angler needs to have as little slack as possible below the strike indicator. If the angler reacts to a jerk on the indicator by twitching the line 6 inches downstream, the hook will be set before the fish realizes it's been duped. Doudy also recommends casting 45 degrees upstream to get the flies down to fish level, then tightening the line as the indicator floats directly across from the angler. As the indicator continues to float past, play out line until the swing, using the lift as it swings back toward the center of the river. (This is also called the Leisenring lift.)

Doudy also varies from conventional wisdom by recommending tying the trailing fly 6 to 8 inches behind the leading fly (instead of 18 to 24 inches).

The BWO hatch will begin in October and can last until mid-November. The midges hatch all year long and, once the BWOs are gone, become the main food source until March.

If nothing else is working, try the old standby of a brown or black Kaufmann Stonefly Nymph #8 to #10 with a green caddis larva dropper #10 to #14. And don't worry about the rig's configuration because, unlike the BWO and midges, trout aren't subtle when they take these flies; they usually hit pretty hard. And don't forget another sure "getter": a peach-colored egg fly and a San Juan Worm such as the IED, both in sizes #10 to #12.

And let's not forget the dry flies, which with BWO hatches on a cloudy day can resemble a fog on the water. A good way to know what the fish are up to during BWO hatches is watching the fish. If their open mouths come out of the water, they are hitting duns. If all you see are fins, they are taking emergers. The trick is to put a dry fly, such as the Blue Dun #18 to #20, on top and drop a gray Sparkle RS-2 #18 to #20 12 to 18 inches below. Cover all the bases.

2. TAYLOR RIVER

This section of the Taylor River begins below Taylor Park Reservoir in the upper Gunnison Basin and runs 20 miles southwest to join the East River at Almont, where they join to become the Gunnison River. The river runs through a canyon as a series of riffles, runs, tumbling rapids, and pools. The town of Gunnison is on US 50, about 3 hours west of Pueblo. From Denver take US 285 southwest to US 50 and head west on US 50 to Gunnison. Almont is 11 miles north of Gunnison on CO 135.

As discussed in the summer section, the Taylor has a split personality. The upper 0.4 mile (a true four-season fishery) is a meadow river with huge, very savvy trout, mostly rainbows. The upper stretch, designated catch-and-release, is technical but rewarding, having produced three state records for rainbows since 2002; the most recent was a 40¼-inch giant with a girth of 29 inches. The upper Taylor is a nice, usually slow run of water that has millions of mysis shrimp pumped into it from the reservoir on a regular basis, so the fish in the upper stretch gorge themselves on the shrimp and don't have to work very hard to eat.

The lower river—a high-running, wild haven for brown trout in the summer, often in the 10- to 15-inch range—by contrast is just too tumultuous for the typical trout to grow very large, and it has just the normal, or a slightly better, number of insect hatches. It's also checkered with private property.

Population
No formal surveys have been done.

Flows
In the fall the Taylor River consistently flows at 75 to 125 cubic feet per second in the tailwater and 150 to 200 c.f.s. in the lower river.

Access
There are many places to park along the 11 miles of public access on the lower river and quite a few on the upper 0.4 mile. Parking areas where you can see the river from the road fill up quickly, and so does the adjacent stretch of water. But there are many fine places to fish that can't be seen from the roadway. Avoid the urge to jump on the first stretch of open water,

and instead, spend some time scouting the river, particularly for pocket water and wading access. It will pay off. The tailwater is flies and lures only, catch-and-release.

Fall Strategy

No matter the season, because of the natural difference between the tailwater and the lower 19.6 miles of the river, two very different strategies are called for. In the fall crowds on the tailwater will have thinned considerably. Nevertheless, stream etiquette suggests the angler stay on the bank or near the bank and not wade into the river.

Find a fish and fish to it, using a good pair of polarized sunglasses. Often the fish will be in front of rocks, enjoying the hydraulic buffer. But look the river over—the fish are there. Most anglers congregate in the large pool below the bridge, but above the bridge and at the tail-out of the pool is also good. I once spooked a big rainbow above the bridge in about a foot of water against a slightly undercut bank. Any fly must be nailed right on the nose of the trout. But these fish reportedly shy away from split shot and even bead head flies.

In the early fall strategy on the lower river is not much different from that for late summer. As the water level drops, most areas will be safely wadable. In warm years, particularly on the lower river, the hatches of summer may still be around in October, but the fish will start keying on the blue-winged olives and fish eggs. Unfortunately, snow and cold in the high country can take the river out of action earlier than most rivers at that altitude. The southeast to northwest orientation and high canyon south wall causes the river to ice over, and big snows can cause road closures because of slides.

> **PRO TIP**
>
> For the spawning browns and any Kokanee salmon, use an egg pattern with a dark nymph trailer, fished deep in pools.

Tactics and Flies

In the tailwater some successful anglers use 14-foot leaders with a fluorocarbon tippet. To get the fly down to fish level, use dull green-colored split shot and nongold bead head flies. With the exception of the green drake hatch in summer, the tailwater fish aren't going to rise to dry flies. In fact, the diet doesn't change much from season to season. Since mysis shrimp are flushed out of the reservoir all year long, a number of shrimp sizes are recommended. For colors stick with white to translucent, with a touch of pink or red to simulate an organism wounded in the dam release tubes, something like Palm's Mysis Shrimp #16. The fish don't generally move much to take a shrimp or a bug, so any movement by the fish, no matter how slight, should be a signal to set the hook—you can see how important good polarized sunglasses are. Drop a midge pattern, such as the Rojo #16 to #22 in red, black, or olive or WD-40 #18 to #22 in gray, black, or brown, off the bend in the hook to double your chances. If a good presentation with your flies isn't working, change flies. Blue-winged olive mayflies will begin hatching in September and will be over by November.

Any mayfly nymph with a midge trailer will make a good combination. If the nymph has a black tungsten bead head, all the better. The next time I fish there, I'm going to try a Peach Egg #14 and the San Juan Worm IED #12. If they work on the San Juan River in New Mexico, they might work on the upper Taylor.

Since the lower Taylor River is almost exclusively a brown trout fishery, take advantage of the fall spawn by using an Egg Fly #14 with the IED #10 combination, or throw a streamer such as the black, brown, or gold Woolly Bugger or Muddler Minnow #10. Let the streamer sink, then bob it along the bottom. For flashier streamers full strip retrieve it over deep holes starting top to bottom at 5-foot intervals, or use the New Zealand method described in the season preview. For BWOs a small mayfly emerger trailed with a midge larva or emerger #18 to #20 should be effective. Kokanee making the run from Blue Mesa Reservoir up the Gunnison sometimes make a wrong turn and end up in the lower part of the lower river. You might find them resting by the hundreds in deep pools in early October. Fish deep with brightly colored nymphs, soft-hackle flies, egg patterns, and streamers. Since these fish are going to die anyway, a limit of 10 fish is allowed.

3. Fryingpan River

The 14-mile stretch of the Fryingpan River is a true four-season fishery because the entire length stays ice free most of the year. It begins at Ruedi Reservoir dam and ends at its confluence with the Roaring Fork River at the town of Basalt, about midway between Aspen and Glenwood Springs. Glenwood Springs is about 2 hours west of Denver on I-70.

With its high populations of large fish, the Fryingpan offers some of the best fishing in the state. But it's especially attractive in the fall when the crowds disperse, and the water releases from the Ruedi Reservoir will average only 80 to 100 cubic feet per second.

Population

A 2010 population survey at the Baetis Bridge (the first bridge below the dam) estimated 1,114 brown trout and 425 rainbow trout per acre at that survey site, with 525 browns and 134 rainbows larger than 14 inches per mile in the same area. Hofer strain rainbows have been stocked in the Fryingpan for 4 years.

An area called the Toilet Bowl, just below the dam, holds trout in the 10- to 15-pound range. The presence of mysis shrimp from the reservoir explains the size of these fish. The upper 2 miles has catch-and-release, fly-and-lure-only restrictions.

Flows

Another plus for the "Pan" in fall is that flows are predictable and fishable in normal precipitation years. With flows averaging 80 to 100 c.f.s. and the crowds dispersed, it's especially attractive in the fall.

Access

Many anglers fish the upper mile because there's easy access and parking, but the fish in the second mile are just a little smaller, and there are fewer anglers. More than 8 miles of the river is open to the public between the town of Basalt and the 2 miles of catch-and-release water below the dam.

Fall Strategy

After all the variables that make summertime fishing so complicated, it's kind of nice to see how simple fall fishing can be. Stream flows are fairly consistent and low enough to safely open up much more of the river, and because of lower flows the fish also tend to concentrate in spots. The crowds are gone, although there will almost always be some anglers around. As in summer, they will mostly be seen in the 2 miles of catch-and-release below the reservoir.

If you've been on the Pan in summer and done some moving around, you've already got an idea as to the layout of the river. If not, the best approach is to find a promising area and work it extensively, not just hitting the big pools but finding the seams and the smaller ones where trout are likely holding. The huge pool known as the Toilet Bowl, just below the dam, is where the huge fish stay fat on mysis shrimp. There are also high numbers of Hofer strain rainbows just below the dam, which should be reaching the 14- to 16-inch range by 2012. In warm, dry Octobers, some pale morning duns, green drakes, and rusty spinner mayflies may be hanging around in the early part of the month. As the weather and water get colder, blue-winged olive mayflies and midges will dominate, and these will be what the fish are keying on. By December the only bugs on the water will likely be midges.

Tiny BWO emergers and flies, such as the RS-2s and WD-40s, effectively imitate both small mayflies and midges if the sizes are correct. Don't forget the streamers and egg patterns, particularly if the fish are reluctant to take tiny bug imitations.

Remember that, while hatches begin at lower elevations when the water warms to approximately 50 degrees, spawning begins in the upper reaches of a river when the water cools to around 50 degrees. On a tailwater such as the Pan, spawning will come down the river fairly quickly. If you see pairs of fish, spawning is in the immediate offing. From then until really cold weather, egg patterns and streamers will bring the best action.

Tactics and Flies

A 9-foot five-weight medium-action rod will work well for most fall fishing on the Pan, but if you are going to throw big, weighted streamers, a 9- to 9½-foot 6W medium-action rod would be better. Medium-action rods (as opposed to fast-action rods) offer more flexibility for casting dry flies and big streamers, and if you do hook up a big fish, the rod's action will help dispel some of the stress on the leaders and tippets.

For the smallest flies you may have to step down to 6X or 7X fluorocarbon tippets, while for the bigger stuff (streamers #10 and larger), a 4X leader and tippet will be necessary. If fishing with streamers is going to

become a regular pastime, use a sink tip or full sink 4 or 5X fly line. If that's unworkable, use a 9-foot 4X leader with a 4X tippet 3 to 4 feet long.

The premier hatch in the fall is blue-winged olive (baetis) mayflies, which starts in early October and can last until early December. Midges are second in numbers and importance as a food source and will begin hatching in the mornings and hit the surface through midday in fair weather. Both will hatch prolifically in overcast weather.

The 2-fly rig, in the mornings when nothing is rising, should have a BWO emerger, such as Barr's BWO Emerger #20 to #24, on top with a Pheasant Tail Nymph or a gray, brown, or black RS-2, both in #20 to #24, or a midge larvae, such as a Black Beauty #22 to #24 or a gray Mercury Midge or Jujubee Midge, both in #22 to #24 and dead-drifted, first with no weight or little weight. Add weight to get them farther down in the water column if they aren't producing strikes near the top. By noon the bugs should be coming off the top. If so, switch to dry flies, such as a standard or Parachute Adams or Mike's Midge, both in #20 to #24, which will work for both BWOs and midges. Midges of several sizes are typically found in the same area, and some of these can get quite large. If you see a bug on the water that looks like a mosquito without its biting apparatus, try to match the size in dry flies, which can be as large as #14.

The prime time to fish with streamers is early mornings and evenings or during cloudy weather. Cast to undercut banks from midstream with a big splash to get a big fish's attention, pause a second, and begin a full strip retrieve, taking in about half your line before recasting. After a few unproductive casts, move down 15 or 20 feet. Cast across pools and runs using the same technique.

Another option is to use the wet-fly (streamer) technique, casting straight across, tight-lining the drift, letting it swing into the current, then lifting the rod to bring the streamer up to the surface.

Because of the tiny flies and correspondingly thin tippets, the buddy system is crucial to landing the largest. Many fish will break off or throw the fly as soon as you get it to within 3 feet of your body. Getting the fish into the net sooner spares the fish from exhaustion that can be fatal, even in the cooler water of fall.

4. Roaring Fork River

A tributary of the Colorado River, the Roaring Fork drains a watershed approximately the size of Rhode Island, flowing 70 miles through alpine meadows, canyons, and the red-rock foothills of the bustling Roaring Fork Valley (home of Aspen, Colorado), to a confluence with the Colorado at Glenwood Springs.

Population

The most recent population studies estimated 2,300 brown trout and 3,000 whitefish in a 2.5-mile stretch below the town of Basalt. As of the late 1990s, whirling disease had all but wiped out the rainbow trout, but with the stocking of the Hofer variety (WD-resistant) rainbows well under way, there should be a resurgence of the rainbow population within a short time.

Flows

Fall is arguably the best time to fish the Roaring Fork River. The flows will average between 100 and 300 cubic feet per second above Basalt, and between 400 and 700 c.f.s. between Basalt and Glenwood Springs, because of the many side streams dumping water into the river. With the wide river channel, these conditions usually make the water easily and safely wadable.

Access

There will likely be a 75 percent reduction in the number of anglers present. Parking at any access is usually possible.

Fall Strategy

As in the summer, a fall fisherman can divide the river into three segments: upper (from Aspen to Basalt), middle (Basalt to Carbondale), and lower (Carbondale to the confluence with the Colorado at Glenwood Springs).

In the fall the upper river can be decidedly fickle, excellent one day and dismal the next. Because of the altitude, the water warms later and cools earlier in the day, which somewhat reduces the size of the insects. The green drakes and PMDs will be gone by October, but the BWOs are just hitting their stride. By December the BWOs will be moving out and midges will have taken over until ice forms on the water. Small flies are the order of the day. These fish are a bit smaller than those in the big water below and don't

Two men in a raft enjoy a quiet float on the Roaring Fork River. Rafts can be one of the best ways to reach tricky stretches of holding water. Kɪʀᴋ Wᴇʙʙ

tend to be too picky (when they are biting). If the ice stays off the water long enough for midges to become the predominant insect the fish are feeding on, use the simple midge patterns. The upper half of the upper Fork below Aspen (about 5.5 miles) is accessible from the Rio Grande (bicycle/pedestrian) Trail and CR 19.

The middle river from Basalt down to Carbondale will produce some late summer insects, such as caddis and PMDs, and some fall insects, such as BWOs and midges in early October. They may last longer in this section, but it'll be all midges in December. As in the upper Fork, small flies are needed—time to start using egg flies and start throwing streamers. The fish are moving to deeper water as the water gets cooler, and fewer fish are holding near the bank. The fishing access adjacent to Basalt remains the hottest spot early in the fall.

October is the time to be on the lower Roaring Fork if you like to catch big fish. BWO emergers are the first choice for flies, but with the brown trout spawn getting underway, go for the gold and use egg flies and streamers. Float trips can be incredibly productive on the lower river because the water and streambed look very uniform from a distance. And it's such a wide river along this stretch that a boat can help the angler cover more water looking for pools. If floating isn't an option, stop at one of the fly shops, get a map, and ask for suggestions and directions to an area.

Tactics and Flies

In the upper river by all means use a dry fly or better yet a tandem dry fly rig with an Elkhair Caddis pattern #14 to #18 on top, followed by a BWO emerger #20 to #24. More likely, the fish will be working below the surface, so use attractor flies, such as Prince Nymphs #18 and Pheasant Tails or Hare's Ears #20 to #24, on a double nymph rig.

From Basalt to Carbondale there may still be healthy numbers of caddis and PMDs in early October, but the BWOs will be the dominant trout food along with midges, which will last until ice-over in December or early January. Look for fish in the deeper pools and seams. A double nymph rig with caddis/BWO emergers using a wet fly technique is best early in the season.

Later a BWO emerger with a midge larva trailer should be effective. Or break out the egg flies and San Juan Worms and streamers for real action. In fact, a double nymph rig with a Peach Egg #16 on top and an IED #12 should be a killer combination. Experiment with weight and depth to get down to the fish.

> ## PRO TIP
>
> "Tandem streamer rigs are lethal when floating the river during the fall months," says Kirk Webb of Taylor Creek Fly Shop. "We often use opposing color schemes with a small streamer trailed by a large streamer to imitate a big fish chasing a smaller fish."

You don't need anything fancy by way of streamers, just a black, brown, or gold bead head Woolly Bugger #8 to #12 or a bead head Autumn Splendor #10 to #12 (which combines brown, orange, and gold). Throw the streamers at undercut banks or across pools, and retrieve with full strips. Cover a pool from top to bottom, near to far, in that order, in 5-foot increments to cover maximum water. When you reach the far side of the pool, tight-line it and let in swing up into the water column, with a lift of the rod tip mimicking the wet fly technique.

5. LAKE FORK OF THE GUNNISON RIVER

The Lake Fork of the Gunnison River's headwaters are in the basin below Red Cloud and Handies Peak, above Lake City, about 50 miles southwest of Gunnison. It flows north through canyons and steep valleys in the upper section into Lake San Cristobal, then through Lake City and north through ranch country into Blue Mesa Reservoir.

A 5-mile stretch of the river through Bureau of Land Management property has had very nice habitat features built into it, greatly increasing the health of the fishery. About 14 miles of public access is available on the section between Lake City and Blue Mesa Reservoir.

The best thing about the Lake Fork is the lack of fishing pressure. Comparable to many other spots in Colorado with quality fishing, the Lake Fork often almost seems deserted. This is especially true in the fall.

Population

The river is whirling disease positive. Rainbow trout reproduction declined between 1998 and 2008, but the Hofer strain of WD-resistant rainbows has been stocked since 2009. In sampled populations brown trout make up about 80 percent of the population, with rainbows the other 20 percent. Per surface acre of water, there are 23 browns and 4 rainbows longer than 14 inches. I caught an 18-inch brownie adjacent to the Gate Campground and saw a 24-inch brown caught under the bridge just upstream from there. There are big fish in this river if the angler is patient.

Flows

Normal flow in the Lake Fork of the Gunnison in the fall is about 80 cubic feet per second. The river typically becomes unfishable because of ice by the middle of November. At the higher altitudes this date may come earlier.

Access

Most of the action is on the lower river, with a short stretch above the Gate Campground. A 5-mile section below the Gates is private. As CO 149 comes off a long hill and turns south, CR 25 turns north. Public access begins about ¼ mile north of there. Because the landowner stocks the river with trophy fish throughout his 5 miles, some of the best fishing begins right at the border to the private land. Don't worry about unintentionally trespassing. The landowner prominently marks his property right at the property line.

From that property line downstream to Blue Mesa Reservoir, it's all public access. The river before Blue Mesa Reservoir is a narrow canyon with cascades and large pools and many places to park.

Fall Strategy

The Lake Fork in the fall sees the unusual situation of blue-winged olive mayflies hatching during the warmest parts of the day, according to Oscar Marks of the Gunnison River Fly Shop.

With the water below 100 c.f.s., the entire river becomes a series of pools where the fish congregate. In the lower river,

> **PRO TIP**
>
> Use a double stonefly nymph rig with unweighted flies.

below the Gate Campground, these pools can be very deep. These are important because Kokanee will run up the Lake Fork from Blue Mesa to spawn. As in the nearby Taylor River, a daily limit of 10 Kokanee is allowed.

Tactics and Flies

A 4W or 5W rod will be sufficient for fishing all but the Kokanee in the deeper pools, where the fish can routinely range from 3 to 5 pounds and fight like banshees once they are hooked. With the BWOs hatching in the middle of the day, use a cripple #16 to #20 BWO spent (spinner) or crippled emerger with a trailing shuck as the top fly and midge larvae, such as a bead head Zebra Midge #18 to #22, as the trailer. Other times go deep with double nymph rigs or an egg pattern leading a small BWO weighted nymph or midge larvae. For the Kokanee use a double nymph rig with bright, flashy colored flies, and for streamers give the Sculpzilla #8 to #10 a try.

NORTHEAST REGION

6. South Platte River in Eleven Mile Canyon

The South Platte River runs through a scenic canyon below the dam on Eleven Mile Reservoir and ends near Lake George on US 24, about 38 miles west of Colorado Springs. The canyon can be reached by turning south on Eleven Mile Canyon Road in Lake George and driving a mile. It features long, slow meanders; riffle/run/pool complexes; deep, lakelike pools and cascades.

Most folks will tell you there aren't any big fish in this section of the South Platte, but once while standing up on the road about 50 feet above the river, I saw a fish that had to be pushing 24 inches swimming next to the bank. Whenever there was movement anywhere near the river, it would disappear beneath the slightly overhanging bank, and then, when things were quiet again, it would come out. Keep an eye out for spots like this when the water is high enough to hide a fish. There's a deep pool about 50 yards downstream where these fish likely take refuge in lower water.

Unfortunately, New Zealand mud snails have also shown up there. These little buggers are hell on fisheries. They successfully compete against insects for the same food, eventually destroying the food base of the aquatic ecosystem, and they reproduce exponentially. Boots and waders must be cleaned to keep the snails from spreading. (See Appendix D for information on controlling the spread of whirling disease and New Zealand mud snails.)

Population

About 2 miles downstream from the dam, the upper catch-and-release section has one of the heaviest concentrations of rainbow trout in the entire state—estimated in 2005 at more than 3,500 trout per mile. Most will be in the 12- to 14-inch range, but 15- to 18-inch rainbows are not uncommon. They are so healthy that they seem much bigger when you are trying to land one. Despite rampant whirling disease, rainbows are now surprisingly populating the lower, nonrestricted 8 miles of river. In the past 20 years, almost no rainbows have reproduced successfully in the entire river system—except in Eleven Mile Canyon.

The only blot on the fishery is the presence of New Zealand mud snails. These little buggers can destroy a fishery because they eat the same microor-

ganisms as insects and, with no natural predators present, reproduce exponentially. Boots and waders must be cleaned to keep the snails from spreading.

Flows
The average fall flow for the river is 50 to 100 cubic feet per second. Flows are
rarely unsafe in the fall.

Access
There is plenty of access along the road in the lower 8 miles of river with
parking lots and pull-offs. In the upper 2 miles, parking is at more of a premium, so arrive early or plan on a short hike. Most of the river will be free of
ice in the fall, but once cold weather settles in, only the area directly below
the dam stays ice free.

Fall Strategy
The average flow for the river in fall, winter, and early spring is about 50
cubic feet per second, making favorable conditions for wading.

The presence of rainbows generally changes the strategy from most
places in Colorado, because rainbows are opportunistic daytime feeders.
And both rainbows and brown trout will go on a feeding frenzy with winter coming on. In the fall blue-winged olives and midges become the fare
of choice. Cloudy weather enhances the hatches of both, but as water gets
colder, direct sunlight on water will bring BWOs to the top. If you're seeing
a lot of fish mouths breaking the surface, they are taking spinners (adults).
If you're seeing a lot of fins but no mouths, they are eating emergers. If there
isn't much surface action at all, go with small nymphs and larvae.

Don't forget that browns, though, will be spawning, and both browns
and rainbows will gobble these eggs as they float downstream. And browns
will attack anything that
annoys them or that comes
close to their spawning beds.

Tactics and Flies
The blue-winged olive mayflies will be in full swing
by early October, and the
midges are always good. Use

> ## PRO TIP
>
> When the water gets low and looks as if it
> might start freezing, tie a weighted streamer
> like a Sculpzilla #4 on a short leader and a
> sinking line, and let it sink all the way to the
> bottom of a deep pool, retrieving it either with
> a half strip or hopping it along the bottom.

a dry on top and a midge dropper or nymph/emerger on top with a midge dropper. Three times out of four, the fish will take the dropper, no matter what is happening on top.

Midges hatch all year long but take a vacation in December and January. As long as the water is open, however, use a 2-fly nymph rig with a mayfly emerger #18 to #20 on top and a weighted Mercury Midge Larvae #20 to #22 on the bottom. If a hatch is on, and adults are on the water and fish are eating them, try a Griffin's Gnat #18 on top with a midge emerger, such as a WD-40 or an RS-2 #20 to #24 as a dropper.

Other great midge patterns are the Rojo Midge #18 to #24 in red and black, the Tungsten Poison Midge, the Brassie #18 to #22, the Black Beauty #18 to #24, and the Jujubee #18 to #24.

Again, don't hesitate to use an egg pattern #12 to #16 in red, pink, or peach along with a worm pattern #10 to #12. I'd suggest one of each size just in case, although I've used the larger size and had great success with them. In other places fish ignore the #12 and insist on the #16. Plastic multiegg patterns are also worth trying.

7. Cache La Poudre River

Beginning 10 miles northwest of Fort Collins and about a mile west of US 287 on CO 14, the Cache La Poudre River canyon runs 70 miles up to Rocky Mountain National Park before reaching the river's headwater. Throughout its length every conceivable type of fishing condition can be found.

Population

In one of the most beautiful canyons in the entire state, recent fish surveys show the highest numbers of large fish—10 to 14 inches—in the Cache La Poudre occur at Indian Meadows. Indeed, the 2006 National Fly Fishing Championship was held in this 5-mile length of river.

The river's rainbow population was decimated by whirling disease in the 1990s. And while brown trout have largely filled many of the habitat niches historically occupied by rainbows, given the new strain of WD–resistant rainbows, this picture should change.

Flows

As always, it varies, but 100 cubic feet per second in early October to 500 c.f.s until early April can be anticipated. The lower rate enables comfortable wading.

Access

Parking is rarely a problem in the fall as there are only about one-quarter the anglers still around compared to in the summer. Wading access is extensive, though many of the pullouts are small, holding only one to two vehicles. Most campgrounds, picnicking sites, and boat put-ins have designated parking spots for anglers. There is some private property far up the canyon where both banks are off limits, but it's well marked and nothing to worry about.

Fall Strategy

With low water the fish are going to be more and more concentrated in deeper holes as the temperature drops, so keep an eye out for these and pick a spot. On warm, sunny days the fish will move to the riffles to feed on midges and emerging blue-winged olive mayflies.

There are two areas that are fly and lure only: The first is about 20 miles up the canyon, from the Pingree Park bridge to the town of Rustic, and the

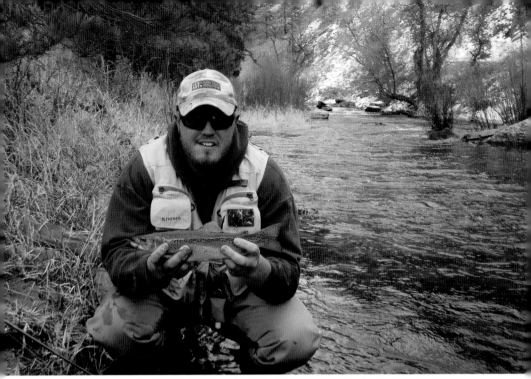

Cory Bolyard holds a still-rare, late-fall rainbow on the Cache La Poudre River.
Jon Spiegel

second begins at Black Hollow Creek, which is just west of Profile Rock and 2 miles east of the old hatchery up to Big Bend Campground.

My favorite place to fish the Poudre is an additional 30 miles from the Big South Fork trailhead, 40 miles up the canyon where the river forks off from Colorado 14. In the fall there are numerous pools that are accessible from the lower segment by following the Big South Trail, but the terrain is steep. Wading this stretch in the fall is possible. Continuing west on CO 14 for about 10 miles to Forest Road 156 (the turnoff to Long Draw Reservoir) and driving an additional 15 miles on a gravel road will put you on the upper river, which is a high-altitude meadow fishery. There is a parking lot at that point that allows access to the headwaters, which lie in a high-altitude meadow with a flatter gradient, trails down both sides of the river, and even a bridge to cross over the river.

The altitude of the upper Big South section of the river is around 10,000 feet and should be open in October, but not much later than that. By November ice will begin forming on the water until the sun comes out. Come December, the ice will be there to stay.

Likewise, the higher elevations of the main stem river (along CO 14) will begin freezing in early November and will be entirely frozen down the confluence of the North Fork of the Poudre at the beginning in the canyon by December. Again, depending upon weather, the river can be ice free through the Poudre River State Wildlife Area at the mouth of the canyon and in the Watson Lake State Wildlife Area/Fish Hatchery just west of the town of Laporte.

This upper section of the Big South Poudre supports healthy populations of rainbow, brown, brook, and cutthroat trout, making it possible for anglers to get a grand slam of trout fishing. The cutts can get to be as large as 16 inches. If the weather is still warm, some of these fish will spread out, but once it gets consistently cold, the fish will congregate in pools and will only be susceptible to nymphs fished deep. The other fish are plentiful but average 10 to 12 inches.

Tactics and Flies

Small rods—an 8.5-foot four-weight, for instance—are perfect for the Poudre River in the fall. Small black stoneflies hatch all fall and winter in the Poudre and are an overlooked insect. BWOs and midges can also be fished, although the BWO hatch will be over by November in most years. Use a double nymph rig with a black or brown K's Stone Fly #8 to #12 on top and an emerger such as Barr's BWO Emerger #18 to #22 as a trailer until the water gets colder. Then keep the stonefly, and switch to a midge larvae such as Rojo Midge, Mercury Midge, Brassie, or Disco Midge #18 to #24 as the trailer. K's Stones are wrapped with lead wire, so no additional weights are necessary.

Since the Poudre is still primarily brown trout water, fall is the time to try egg flies and streamers. Spawning begins when the water temperature drops below 50 degrees, so the spawn necessarily begins at higher altitude first. Try a double egg fly tandem in a size #12 on top and #16 on the bottom—in different colors. If fish don't respond, you may be too far below the spawn. For streamers use a Vanilla Woolly Bugger, or an olive, brown, or black Woolly Bugger #8 to #12.

8. Big Thompson River below Estes Park

The Big Thompson River below Lake Estes in Estes Park winds 20 miles down a canyon into the city of Loveland, which is in turn about 50 miles north of Denver on US 287 or I-25. From Loveland take US 34 west to the mouth of the canyon.

A major flood in 1976 destroyed much of the canyon, resulting in a habitat restoration effort that created one of the most productive trout fisheries on the Front Range.

Population
Despite the presence of whirling disease organisms, the Big Thompson is one of only two rivers in the state to have a healthy reproducing rainbow trout population. A 2009 survey in a 572-foot section of the Big Thompson below Olympus Dam estimated there were 149 rainbows and 112 brown trout larger than 6 inches, with the most common sizes being 12 to 14 inches. Some fish were as large as 16 inches. A 24-inch brown was captured in 2009 during a fish survey, close to a popular picnic ground in the lower river.

Flows
Fall flows average 40 to 60 c.f.s., making the water manageable from a wading standpoint and tending to concentrate fish into pools.

Access
Parking is not a problem in the fall. About half a mile of river below the dam stays ice free most of the winter, but by late December most of the rest of the river will be iced over. When the river is covered with ice, the tailwater section below the dam can become very crowded.

Fall Strategy
As in the nearby Cache La Poudre, the fall angler will find midges, blue-winged olive mayflies, and stoneflies, with the BWOs tailing off in early November. And again, the brown trout will be spawning, so it's worth trying egg patterns and streamers. As the water cools, fish will move toward pools and deep runs. If you spot a fish holding on a sandy bottom but not being very active, go ahead and cast to it, but be careful not to walk through the spawning bed, which is a real danger when the water gets low. As a rule the

Two anglers check the water in order to better place their flies. Jon Spiegel

fish are larger and slightly more numerous above the Waltonia Bridge, which is the lower boundary of the catch-and-release section.

Tactics and Flies

Any standard size or length of fly rod will work in low water in the fall. If possible, use a high-floating, light-colored fly line or tipped fly line, such as a Rio Gold, and use it as a strike indicator. These fish are strike-indicator shy.

Early in the fall overcast days will stimulate BWO and midge hatches, but as the water gets colder, warm, sunny days will bring the bugs to the top. As in most trout streams, stoneflies will be present in the nymph form. They are not large and are dark colored. Fish are always looking for a meal the size of a stonefly, and I've had success with a number of smaller nymph patterns #10 to #14. When a BWO hatch is on, tie an olive black or brown RS-2 #18 to #22 and fish it as a dry fly. Fish will almost always

PRO TIP

About 2 miles up the canyon, there is a water diversion and a parking area on the south side of the highway. From the parking area to where the river crosses under the road (about ¼ mile), there is excellent fishing for rainbows and browns up to 14 inches. Riprap along the elevated highway makes hiking along the river difficult, but it's well worth the effort.

take an emerger floating just beneath the surface over a fly on top.

When the BWOs are gone, try a 2-fly rig with a small stonefly nymph on top trailed by a Mercury Midge or Black Beauty midge larva #18 to #20 beneath either the dry or nymph.

When fishing the tailwater, use the same combinations as above (except for the stoneflies), and downsize the flies to compensate for the year-round colder temperatures.

NORTHWEST REGION

11. Blue River

The Blue River looks like a small mountain stream until it reaches the valley above Breckenridge and starts meandering (with a number of trout habitat improvements) toward Dillon Reservoir. Below the reservoir many habitat improvements have been built in the first 2 miles, and the channel is relatively wide, making much of the tailwater wadable, except during peak run-off. The 15-mile stretch from the tailwater to Green Mountain Reservoir is a classic, mountain valley river, with riffle/run/pool complexes throughout and many large and very large boulders in the water.

Population
With huge fish below the dam in Silverthorne (rainbows and browns up to 30 inches and 10 pounds), big fish coming into the river to spawn from Green Mountain Reservoir, and many nice if somewhat fickle fish between 10 and 14 inches the rest of the time, who can complain about the lack of a fish census in recent years? Even though the river is whirling disease positive, as in most other fishing spots in Colorado, it's being stocked with WD-resistant rainbows.

Flows
Historic flows in the fall average 50 to 100 cubic feet per second, a relatively meager flow that will concentrate fish into pools..

Access
There is excellent access on the river above Dillon Reservoir, by the tailwater section, and downstream to Green Mountain Reservoir and below. The access points are usually near habitat improvements or generally fine stretches of fishing water. The first access is the Blue River Campground, which is 6 miles from Silverthorne. Sutton Unit State Wildlife Area is 7 miles from town, Eagle's Nest Wildlife Area is 9 miles, and the Blue River Wildlife Area 17 miles. Most of the river above Dillon Reservoir and adjacent to Breckenridge is along the highway and has a bike/pedestrian path. The areas that are private are clearly marked.

Fall is a great time to be on the Blue River for the scenery as well as for the fishing. Jon Spiegel

Fall Strategy

In the freestone section fall sees an influx of Kokanee salmon and spawning brown trout from Green Mountain Reservoir. Egg patterns and San Juan worms are productive, as are highly colored streamers and flies. Given a biannual blue-winged olive hatch and ongoing midge hatches, a successful angler has to be prepared for almost anything and be willing to try different combinations of flies, weights, and line length below the strike indicator for success. Several of the better public accesses are situated near Green Mountain Reservoir and should be tried first. Of course, in the tailwater below the dam, shrimp patterns and tiny midges will still be the action for the bruisers there. The successful anglers are the ones who fish this stretch regularly, can sight-fish to specific fish, and create a natural presentation over and over again. Anything that looks suspicious, including shiny split shot or beads, drifts that are too fast or too slow, and line flash and splash, will put a fish down. Set the hook gently when you see a fish move slightly to one side or the other or up in the water column, or just open its mouth. Then be ready for a fight.

Tactics and Flies

While the action below the dam will still require 6X and 7X tippets, unobtrusive strike indicators, and precise drifts of tiny mysis shrimp or midge patterns, the formula for downstream will be based more on observations. For San Juan worms, such as the IED #12, and various colored (peach is my favorite) egg flies #14 to #16, and maybe even #18 BWO patterns, 5X leaders and/or tippets will be fine. If you get into the streamers, 3X or 4X leaders and tippets will be required.

Early in the season look for the BWOs to rise in the slower runs and pools, and use a dry fly, such as a Paradun BWO #18 on top and a gray sparkle RS-2 #18 to #20 or a Mercury BWO #18 to #22 as a trailing emerger, especially on overcast days. Later in October, when the BWOs are starting to fade away, drop a Tung Zebra #18 to #20 or Rojo Midge #16 to #20. By November and December use a midge dry, such as Griffin's Gnat (which imitates a cluster of midges), on top, and drop a Jujubee Midge #20 to #24 or Craven's Poison Tung #20 to #24. Tungsten beads are important for getting your fly down to the fish when they're split shot shy. For indicator-shy fish try the Thingamabobber indicator in white. It's a plastic ball with air. It looks like an air bubble and shouldn't scare the fish.

The Kokanee will run various distances up the Blue River from Green Mountain Reservoir starting in September, adding another dimension to fishing in the fall. They typically run at night and rest in deep pools during the day. Once there, they are vulnerable to flashy fly patterns, possibly because of aggravation. Streamer patterns #6 to #10 with pink or Krystal Flash, chartreuse Copper Johns, Flashback Pheasant Tails, and Prince Nymphs, all #10 to #12, seem to suitably aggravate these landlocked salmon to strike. Regulations allow 10 of these fish to be kept by anglers, probably because they are going to die after eggs are laid and fertilized.

PRO TIP

Try a double egg fly setup with enough weight to keep them near the bottom. If a Kokanee doesn't take it, a brown trout likely will.

12. Williams Fork River below Williams Fork Reservoir

The Williams Fork River tailwater is a 2-mile section of river near the town of Parshall on US 40, between the towns of Hot Sulphur Springs and Kremmling. Beginning at the dam below Williams Fork Reservoir and ending at the confluence with the Colorado River, there are riffles, runs, and deep pools, with undercut banks in narrow spots.

Population

While angler reports have consistently reported good fishing, with the average trout size being about 14 inches, water diversions have reportedly destroyed much of the salmon fly habitat in the nearby Colorado River. Further diversions of water to the Front Range are currently being planned. For now, however, the fishing is holding steady.

Flows

Autumn sees periodic low flows of the river from 75 to 120 cubic feet per second, an excellent rate for fishing.

Access

Access to the river can be gained by turning south at Parshall on CR 3 for 1 mile to a parking area for river access. The hike is about a mile. When the Colorado River is wadable, go to the first access west of Parshall, cross the river, and walk east to the confluence of the Williams Fork and Colorado rivers, then work upstream. It can get pretty cold and windy, so take a backpack with clothes, food, and drink, to stay comfortable.

Fall Strategy

In October the fish may still be holding in the faster water, such as riffles, edges of runs, and pocket water, instead of in pools. As the weather and water get colder, they will eventually move to the deep pools—or someplace in between. You may have to adjust your rig a couple of times to fish different water to find where the fish are. By December, however, they will all be holding in the deepest holes. Or they could be holding deep, then be drawn to the riffle water on sunny days to take advantage of short BWO hatches.

As fall spawners, brown trout turn aggressive and can often be attracted to a strategically stripped streamer. RUSSELL MILLER

Depending on the weather, the BWOs will be mostly gone by early to mid-November, and midges will be the only bugs in the water.

Tactics and Flies

Standard 9-foot 5W rods are fine for almost all fishing on the Williams in the fall, and a 6X tippet will be needed for flies to mimic blue-winged olives and midges, the primary hatches from October to January. Blue-winged olives will be hatching beginning in mid-September. If there is one hatch that stirs the kind of excitement anglers dream about, it's the BWO hatches in spring and late summer / early fall.

Most anglers use a dry/dropper setup for the runs and riffles or an emerger/nymph setup with plenty of weight for the deep pools. Be different and replace your dry flies with an unweighted emerger, such as Barr's BWO Emerger #18 to #24, and tie on a Pheasant Tail Nymph #20 to #22. If this doesn't work, add a little weight between the flies about 6 inches above the bottom fly, and keep adding weight and adjusting your strike indicator until you can dredge the deep pools. The split shot should be bouncing on the bottom from time to time, if you have the proper weight and strike indicator position. By late November these flies should be appropriate midge imitations, which will probably require going down one size all the way around.

As cold as the water is coming out of the reservoir, brown trout spawning should come fairly early. It's worth a try to use an egg fly/San Juan Worm #12 to #16 combination almost any time, and even if the fish don't take the egg pattern, use it on top to get a fish's attention, and trail a BWO or midge, so they've got something to bite on.

SOUTHEAST REGION

13. Arkansas River

Starting southwest of Leadville, the Arkansas flows for 150 miles before emptying into the plains east of Pueblo. Almost all of it is open to floating, but only about 75 miles is open to foot access—more than enough for a lifetime of fishing.

The size and diversity of the water makes it difficult to fish, but with lower flows in the fall, the Arkansas becomes almost like a pussycat instead of a tiger. Short of your falling in and having a heart attack because of the cold water, it's not very dangerous. The crowds are gone, and the fish are hungry.

Population

There are no formal fish population surveys on the whole of the Arkansas, but you'll find many stretches with incredible numbers of brown trout. And it's only getting better. Mine tailings that had been polluting the river and stunting the growth of fish have been largely curtailed. Using Division of Wildlife surveys and the number of fish that rise to the surface during the blanket caddis hatches, outfitter/guide Bill Edrington of Royal Gorge Anglers in Cañon City estimates as many as 4,000 brown trout per mile in many stretches of the river between Salida and Cañon City. Above Salida there are still plenty of fish, but possibly not as many because of the fast current in the canyons.

Flows

Between October and March the flows run from 250 to 400 cubic feet per second, meaning that, while there will be plenty of spots deep enough for a dunking, the current probably won't wash you to Pueblo.

Access

The Arkansas River is managed by the Arkansas Headwaters Recreation Association, a consortium of local, state, and federal agencies, and this group has produced a detailed and accurate map of the river and public access areas. It is given away locally at businesses along the river and by the

PRO TIP

The fall BWO hatch is the third-best dry fly fishing on the Arkansas of the year.

Arkansas Headwaters Recreation Area at 307 W. Sackett, Salida, CO 81201.

Some of the nicest weather of the year shows up in October. Parking should never be a problem in the fall.

Fall Strategy

As mentioned in the summer section, Bill Edrington's book, *Fly Fishing the Arkansas,* is an invaluable resource for understanding the river. Much of my information comes from his work.

The Arkansas can be divided into several sections. The first section, moving from upstream to downstream, is accessed at the Hayden Ranch, beginning at the US 24 bridge about 8 miles south of Leadville and extending 5 miles downstream to the Granite access. The next section is from Granite down to Buena Vista, the third from Buena Vista to Salida, the fourth from Salida to Cañon City, and the fifth below Pueblo Reservoir through the city of Pueblo.

By October the Hayden Ranch stretch of river is low and cold and not particularly productive. The river from the bottom of Hayden Ranch to Balltown (just above Twin Lakes Reservoir outlet) is physically more varied and includes riffles, runs, and pools, but it sits at about 9,000 feet and so it cools early.

The river from Balltown to Buena Vista squeezes runs through a canyon with some public access. Since it's a north-south canyon, it picks up enough sunlight to warm the water. It has a lot of deep pools and is worth checking out.

Below Buena Vista down to Salida, the river includes Browns Canyon (one of the wildest, hairiest stretches of water anywhere), but between Buena Vista and Browns Canyon, and again from below Browns Canyon to Salida, the river is wide and meandering, with manageable banks in most places.

From Salida downstream to Cañon City, the fishing gets interesting. Access is maximized and clearly designated. There are some official public parking areas with such amenities as restroom facilities, boat ramps, and picnic areas. The area directly downstream from Salida is Gold Medal Water, and most of it is open on at least one bank. This trend is true only up to the Royal Gorge. In the gorge the water is too fast to fish safely and, with the rocky streambed providing little vegetation for aquatic insects, generally poor fishing.

In Cañon City a trail with benches and outhouses follows the river. Below Cañon City, there is no river fishing access until below the dam at Pueblo Reservoir. The river through the town of Pueblo has become one of the most popular areas for winter fishing because of some excellent habitat improvements and regular stocking of rainbow trout.

Tactics and Flies

In addition to the attractor flies recommended in the summer (flies such as the Yellow Humpy, Royal Wulff, Renegade, and Royal Coachman Trude

A fish rises to the surface to take a late season BWO on the Arkansas River.
RUSSELL MILLER

on top and nymphs such as Pheasant Tails, Hare's Ears, and Prince Nymphs as the droppers), in October be on the lookout for the smallish, gray blue-winged olive mayflies. These will become the trout's primary food source going into winter. They will usually show up in early October and be gone by late December as the river freezes. The hatches occur early in the day, and the BWOs lay their eggs in the evenings, when the weather turns warm, but should move more toward the middle of the day as the water cools. With quite a bit of flat water around, this is prime dry-fly time. Put a standard Parachute Adams or a Parawulff BWO, both in sizes #16 to #20, as your top fly and a bead head Pheasant Tail nymph #16 to #20 or an olive bead head Hare's Ear #16 to #20 as your dropper, weighted enough to get down into pools but not necessarily on the bottom, as these tiny flies will get caught in the current and can be at any depth.

FALL SEASON SUMMARY

It's hard to go wrong fishing Colorado in the fall. The weather is clear and crisp, the fish are hungry, and the bugs are coming off the water. My three top fall choices—the Blue River, the Taylor River, and the Lake Fork of the Gunnison—all have fall runs of Kokanee salmon, adding an additional dimension to your fishing options. These fish give you a chance to use those gaudy streamers and nymphs that you bought before you knew better. You know, the ones you have in a box at the back of your closet lest your angler friends see them. And they might just work for brown trout, too. There are no bad choices this time of the year, just bad timing. Check with a local fly shop for the most current information on hatches, stream flow, and types of flies to use.

WINTER

One thought to keep in mind about Colorado winter fishing: Like the Boy Scouts, be prepared! Another thought? It's not for everybody, but some folks love it.

First comes the decision on whether or not to even go. Bill Edrington, proprietor of Royal Gorge Anglers in Cañon City, uses the 3-day rule: If the highs are above freezing for 3 days, he goes. He suggests layered clothing,

Winter fishing on the Blue River can be rewarding on any number of levels.
TIM ROMANO

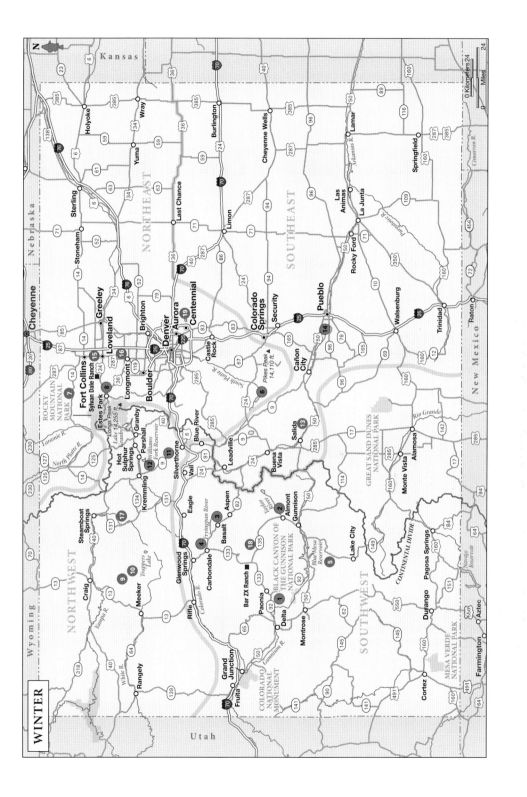

starting with microfleece long johns and SmartWool socks, along with a midweight underwear top, a shirt, a fleece vest, a Gore-Tex jacket, and something to protect your head and ears, as well as fishing gloves. Everything should be breathable and moisture wicking. At the river put on breathable chest waders and boots, and add a wading belt and staff. Get a few chemical hand warmers. They are inexpensive, safe, effective, and a great help if you have to tie a #26 or #28 midge on a 7X tippet.

And speaking of boots, if you are walking in snow, felt soles will pick up so much of it that it will be like hiking with concrete slabs on your feet. Consider soft rubber soles as alternatives.

You will also need a deicing product such as Stanley's Ice-Off Paste for the guides on your fly rod. You might even consider taking a "beater" rod in case it breaks in the cold. Depending on how far you are driving, take a "survival" kit with you—tire chains, extra warm clothes, food, and water. Take thermoses of hot cider and soup if you're planning on more than a couple of hours of fishing, and don't forget the sunglasses, and ... and ... you get the picture.

On the other hand, your fly selection is greatly simplified: golden stone nymphs and midge larvae emergers and dry flies. The timing, too, is simple. Fish in the warmest part of the day. Sunshine is good in winter fishing: Even the rivers that never freeze over will get slushy in the coldest weather, and an hour of sunshine will often melt the slush.

SOUTHWEST REGION

1. Gunnison River in Gunnison Gorge

Beginning at Black Canyon National Park upstream and ending at the confluence of the North Fork of the Gunnison River east of Delta, Colorado, the Gunnison River in the gorge may well be one of Colorado's most difficult big waters to reach. This is especially true in the winter, a time of year when there are only two ways in—by watercraft or by wading or ferrying across the North Fork of the Gunnison at Pleasure Park, above the North Fork's confluence with the Gunnison. The roads to the four trailheads in the upper river often become impassable in the winter. Although anglers can hike to the trailheads and down into the gorge, it's a long round-trip, especially with winter gear. The trails are steep and can be hazardous. A safer bet is the Smith Fork trail beginning at Pleasure Park and crossing the North Fork of the Gunnison to get onto the northeast bank.

It may not be easy but thousands of anglers make the trip every year. It's not hard to understand why—with its staggering scenery and extremely high trout populations—this may well be the crown jewel of Colorado trout fishing.

Population

As I have pointed out in earlier sections, a 2005 fish census estimated an astounding average 7,000 brown trout per mile throughout the 14-mile length of the Gunnison Gorge, excluding the Black Canyon of the Gunnison. Many of those fish are in the 15- to 18-inch range. The largest were 24 to 27 inches long.

Flows

Water releases in January and February average 500 cubic feet per second, above which it is considered unsafe to wade.

Access

To get to Pleasure Park, drive about 12 miles east of Delta on CO 92. The North Fork is often dewatered by irrigation in the summer and quite a bit lower than the main stem Gunnison. There is a 4-mile-long trail along the

Who says winter is a bad time to fish? Angler Willie Tiefel doesn't believe it. JON SPIEGEL

northeast bank of the river once you are across. This is known as the Smith Fork Trail. The bank is manageable on this side and allows greater access to the river. The river is wider and shallower in the first few miles above the confluence than upstream and is therefore more likely wadable. Even in the lower flows of winter, anglers are encouraged to wear a wading belt, have a wading staff, and wear studded felt or rubber soles for safety anywhere on the river.

Winter Strategy

Fishing the Gunnison Gorge in the winter can be intimidating. It isn't often that I suggest anglers hire a float guide/outfitter to fish. For the Gunnison, however, I do—especially for a first-time angler in these waters (in any season). A single float trip is all you would need to learn enough to return on your own. There are too many variables for a first-time angler to have much chance of a successful fishing experience on a one-day trip into the gorge his or her first time out.

But if you decide to hike, take some comfort in the fact that the slower current in the rivers is near the banks, and that's where most of the fish will be holding. Look for any slick water to cast to because those will be the slowest spots.

Tactics and Flies

Heavier rods are a good idea on this big water because they expand your casting range. Set your indicator, weight, and flies up, according to the Gale Doudy method described in the Gunnison Gorge fall "Tactics and Flies" section. Midges will be the only insects that are actively hatching in the winter, but if there are no visible hatches, you can safely assume there are plenty of midge larvae and emergers in the water. The same with stoneflies. Put the weighted stonefly on top and an unweighted or weighted midge on the bottom. Try a Bitch Creek or a Half Back #6 to #10 for the stonefly and a lighter colored RS-2 or a Rojo Midge #16 to #20 for the trailing fly. My old favorite rig of an egg fly #12 to #16 and a red or orange San Juan Worm #12 to #16 will take fish. If you want to fish streamers, use a light-colored or white fly #6 to #10 and full strip in through the smooth spots.

2. Taylor River

This section of the Taylor River begins below Taylor Park Reservoir in the upper Gunnison Basin and runs 20 miles southwest to join the East River at Almont, where they join to become the Gunnison River. The town of Gunnison is on US 50, about 3 hours west of Pueblo. From Denver take US 285 southwest to US 50, and head west on US 50 to Gunnison. Almont is 11 miles north of Gunnison on CO 135.

Winter fishing begins below Taylor Park Reservoir in the upper Gunnison Basin and runs for 0.4 mile before it hits private water. The lower 20 miles of river is frozen during most winters.

Population
The upper 0.4 mile (a true four-season fishery) is a meadow river with giant, well-educated trout, mostly rainbows. The upper stretch of the Taylor River (which is catch-and-release) is the most technical but is ultimately the most rewarding: It has produced three state records for rainbows since 2002.

Flows
The Taylor River flows at about 75 cubic feet per second below the dam in January and February, but anglers are nevertheless asked to fish from the bank.

Access
There are many parking spaces on the upper 0.4 mile of the tailwater. The road up has been known to be covered with snow and rock slides in the winter, so travelers should check with local authorities or businesses in Almont before making the drive. I think this is probably the highest altitude major fishery in the state, maybe in the country, and the winter weather can become brutally cold and even worse when the wind is blowing. Taylor Park, just up the road, has recorded 60 below when the wind wasn't blowing. Having quick access to a vehicle that will start could be a lifesaver. On the other hand, you might get temperatures as high as 30 degrees and sunny conditions—but you may not know until you get there.

Winter Strategy
Since the snow accumulation at Taylor Park can get roof high, wear light-colored clothes to blend with the background. The water should be very

clear, so sight-fishing is possible. If
it gets a little green, just find a likely
holding area, and fish to that. These
fish are thought to shy from highly
colorful strike indicators, split shot,
and shiny bead head flies, which
presents a real challenge to anglers.
Using flies with dull-colored tung-

sten beads is one alternative. Another is Dinsmore split shot, which is camo
green. These are made from both tin and lead; the tin split shot requires a
real squeeze to stay on the leader or tippet, but it's better for the fishery and
the fish. Attach weight 16 inches or more above the top fly. And add weight
to get your flies down by using several small shot instead of one large one.
There seems to be an ongoing debate about whether fluorocarbon or monofilament tippets are best, probably because a hooked fish will try to break
the line by dragging it across rocks in the stream. Use whichever one you're
comfortable with.

Leader/tippet lengths of 12 feet are generally preferred. Some of the
most successful anglers on the Taylor tailwater use leaders/tippets as long
as 15 feet. A 5X tippet is standard, but 6X will be necessary for flies as small
as size #20.

Tactics and Flies

The standard rods in this spot are 9- to 9½-foot 5W and 6W. Fish don't move
much in this cold water, so a natural drift is critical, and the hook should be set
as soon as a fish in proximity to your flies moves or even opens its mouth. Set
the hook by flipping the rod tip in a short arc downstream, with the tip finishing just above the water. Flies on tailwaters should be a size smaller than you'd
use on freestone rivers. Nymph larvae patterns should #18 to #24, and mysis
shrimp patterns should be #16 to #20. Epoxy Baetis, Olive Sparkle RS-2s, and
red and black Palomino Midges are favored by old-timers at this site.

Pheasant Tail Nymphs; Barr's BWO and PMD Emergers; black, red,
olive, and purple Rojo Midges; Brassies; (two-toned) Tungsten Zebra Midges
in red/black and purple/red; and glass bead WD-40s are all effective. But
don't show up there without a handful of mysis shrimp patterns, as consensus is that it's the most effective pattern. Some of the favorites are Sand's
Epoxy Mysis, BTS, Reid's Ultra, and Pacific Fly Mysis.

3. Fryingpan River

From the Toilet Bowl just below Ruedi Reservoir to its confluence with the Roaring Fork River at the town of Basalt, the Fryingpan River stays free of ice for most of the year. And while the largest fish congregate just below the dam, growing fat on mysis shrimp from the reservoir, there are rainbows and browns throughout the watercourse.

Population
A 2010 population survey at the Baetis Bridge (the first bridge below the dam) estimated 1,114 brown trout and 425 rainbow trout per acre at that survey site, with 525 browns and 134 rainbows larger than 14 inches per mile in the same area. Hofer strain rainbows have been stocked in the Fryingpan for 4 years.

Just below the dam, the Toilet Bowl holds trout in the 10- to 15-pound range. The presence of mysis shrimp from the reservoir explains the size of these fish. The upper 2 miles has catch-and-release, fly-and-lure-only restrictions.

Flows
Winter releases from Ruedi Reservoir average about 75 cubic feet per second. In the coldest weather the water in the lower river will become slushy during the night but will clear up during the warmest part of the day.

Access
Many anglers fish the upper mile, given its easy access and parking, but the fish populations in the second mile are only a little less than the upper mile, and fewer anglers are on that water. Access to the lower river is plentiful, with more than 8 miles open to the public between the town of Basalt and the 2 miles of catch-and-release water below the dam. Parking is not a problem in the winter.

Winter Strategy
The cold air temperature, along with low flows, becomes a strategic concern in the winter on the Fryingpan. The valley gets little light because of the high valley walls, and anchor ice and ice channels can pretty much eliminate fishing until things warm up a bit. Look for sunny stretches of river, though, and

you might see midges hatching. But the sun does hit the area beneath the dam where the valley widens out.

In the colder months the largest fish in the river will tend to hold in the slower current, while smaller fish will be more spread out (albeit still concentrated in the slower water). If the water warms only to a high of 33 to 34 degrees, the fish will be lethargic and will not move laterally. Sight-fishing is a must. Higher flows and warmer air temperatures can reverse things quickly and even stimulate midge hatches. In that case ideal weather would be 20 degrees and above with overcast skies.

Tiny BWO emergers and flies such as the RS-22 and WD-40 effectively imitate both small mayflies and midges if the size and color are correct. But don't forget the streamers and egg patterns, particularly if the fish are not taking tiny bug imitations.

Tactics and Flies

If fishing small dries, you may need to step down to 6X or 7X fluorocarbon tippets. At times the flies on the water may be as small as #30. This presents a problem for some, because of the dexterity required to tie on such small flies with cold fingers. Midges, mysis shrimp, and eggs are the most important food sources, with shrimp being more important in the tailwater area and less important the farther you get downstream. For midges use a gray, brown, or black RS-2 #20 to #30 or a midge larvae, such as a Black Beauty #22 to #30 or a gray Mercury Midge or Jujubee Midge #22 to #30. Dead-drift them first with no weight or little weight. If there are no strikes near the top, start adding weight to get them farther down in the water column. Midges of several sizes are typically found in the same area, and some of these can get quite large. If you see a bug on the water that looks like a mosquito (without a biting apparatus), try to match its size, going up to as large as #16. Dry flies, such as Matt's Midge #10 to #20, Griffin's Gnat #16 to #22, and Sprout Midge #16 to #20, are effective when trout rise to the surface and show their mouths. In low light situations in temperatures above freezing, try small streamers such as black, brown, and olive Woolly Buggers #10 to #12.

4. Roaring Fork River

Starting at 12,000 feet, much of the Roaring Fork River's 70-mile run is unfishable in the winter. But beginning at the town of Basalt (elevation, 6,611 feet), there is some fine dry fly and streamer fishing for the intrepid angler.

Population
In a 2.5-mile stretch below the town of Basalt, a census found 2,300 brown trout and 3,000 whitefish. As of the late 1990s, whirling disease had all but wiped out the rainbow population, but with the stocking of WD-resistant rainbows well under way, there should shortly be a resurgence.

Flows
The water flows will be around 250 cubic feet per second at Basalt and 450 c.f.s. at Glenwood Springs.

Access
Because there are quite a few hard-to-find access sites, grab a local map to guide you. There will likely be more anglers than you expect fishing the Roaring Fork in the winter but not as many as in the summer and not enough to affect the fishing access.

Winter Strategy
From late November almost all fishing on the Fork will be between Basalt and Glenwood Springs. Sometimes the water will be slushy in the morning but clear in the afternoon. In warm years the river above Basalt will open up at times. Check at a local fly shop for current information.

Tactics and Flies
A 9-foot 5W rod is plenty for this stretch of river. In the river between Basalt and Carbondale, the fish will be sitting in slow water, lethargically feeding on midges and blue-winged olive nymphs. Use a double nymph rig with a weighted stonefly nymph, such as a 20-incher or a Poxyback Golden, and a midge larvae or emerger, such as a black, brown, or gray RS-2. The key is getting the flies down to the fish because they won't move very far. Find a pool or a deep run, and keep adding weight until the flies are ticking the bottom.

Below Carbondale use the same flies but step the size of the stonefly up a notch or two. Egg flies, such as the Flashtail Mini Egg #16, can be substituted for the midge. A Flash Prince or Tung Prince #12 can be substituted for the stonefly. Whitefish, considered a nuisance by some trout anglers, are actually quite tasty when smoked and even put up a decent fight. They eat the same aquatic insects as trout. There is no bag limit for whitefish in Colorado.

NORTHEAST REGION

6. South Platte River in Eleven Mile Canyon

This stretch of the South Platte River runs through a scenic canyon below the dam on Eleven Mile Reservoir and ends near Lake George on US 24, about 38 miles west of Colorado Springs. The canyon can be reached by turning south on Eleven Mile Canyon Road in Lake George and driving 1 mile. It features long, slow meanders; riffle/run/pool complexes; and deep, lakelike pools and cascades.

The roads in the canyon are plowed regularly, but they are gravel, so there may be a thin layer of snow. With no hills to deal with, all-season tires should be plenty to get around. As a bonus a little snow helps keep the dust down, which can be obnoxious in the summer and fall. However, if it is snowing heavily, the road may not be plowed until the snow stops.

Population

The upper catch-and-release section (stretching about 2 miles downstream from the dam) has one of the heaviest concentrations of rainbow trout in the entire state. A fish population survey in 2005 estimated there were more than 3,500 trout per mile here. Most will be in the 12- to 14-inch range, but larger fish are not uncommon. They are so healthy that they seem much bigger when you are trying to land one. Despite whirling disease, rainbows are now populating the lower, nonrestricted 8 miles of river. In the past 20 years, almost no rainbows have reproduced successfully in the entire river system—except in Eleven Mile Canyon.

New Zealand mud snails are present here, which can destroy the fishery. With no natural predators, the snails reproduce exponentially, and they reduce the fish's food source, by feeding on the same microorganisms eaten by insects. Boots and waders must be cleaned to keep the snails from spreading.

Flows

From November to March, flow is between 40 and 60 cubic feet per second. Only the first mile below the dam is not covered with ice.

Access

In the upper 2 miles, what is limited parking in summer seems to be plenty for the smaller number of winter anglers.

Winter Strategy

In January and February only the area directly below the dam stays free of ice. It's a simpler fishery, reduced to a relatively short stretch and with a small amount of water. In the fall, winter, and early spring, the flow is only about 50 cubic feet per second, so the riffle/run/pool complexes aren't quite as complex as they are during the summer.

The presence of rainbows in Eleven Mile Canyon doesn't mean as much in the winter as it does the other three seasons, partially because the slow water right below the dam is prime brown trout habitat; rainbows tend to stay in faster water. A brutal series of cascades between the slower water near the dam and the riffle/pool/run water downstream tends to keep the rainbows out of the tailwater pool.

Tactics and Flies

The quiet January is more than made up for in February. The South Platte River in the canyon is known for its early season dry fly fishing. Midges lead the way, hatching for several hours a day. But long leaders and 7X tippets and tiny flies are necessary to fool the trout. Parachute Adams #26, Matt's Midge #24, and Griffin's Gnat #24 are the dry flies of choice. When nothing is hatching, use midge larvae #24 to #26 to sight-fish trout in slow, deep pools. If you haven't worked with 7X tippet and #26 flies, well, it's a real challenge, requiring high-magnification glasses and nimble fingers. An apt analogy would be trying to tie a broken pencil tip with a strand of spider web. A 9-foot 5W is plenty of rod for this stretch of river, but the 5X tippet will have to be stepped down to 6X, then 7X to get a good drift.

> **PRO TIP**
>
> You may have noticed, especially in the winter, that the same flies keep popping up. Many of these flies sell for just a few dollars apiece, often because the names are patented. But it's a hazy legal issue, and if you go online, you can often find the same flies, with a slightly different name or a tiny design change for even less, especially in bulk. If you go in with friends, this is an affordable option. The trick is that you have to know what the flies look like. In many cases the names and designs are indistinguishable from the patented ones, but in others the design is the same and the names are different. In some cases the quality isn't as good, but there is no way to tell until you fish with them. If you plan to fish a lot, though, it's an option worth considering.

8. Big Thompson River below Estes Park

The Big Thompson River below Estes Park winds for 20 miles down a canyon into the city of Loveland. Depending upon the weather, 0.5 to 1 mile of river is free from ice in January and February. Although the spot is sheltered by the Lake Estes dam, winds from Rocky Mountain National Park often roar through the town, creating crosswinds and making casting difficult. Check the weather report for Estes Park before driving up.

Population
While whirling disease is present, the Big Thompson is one of only two rivers in the state to have a healthy reproducing rainbow trout population. A trout population survey in a 572-foot section of the Big Thompson below Olympus Dam in 2009 estimated there were 149 rainbows and 112 brown trout larger than 6 inches, with the most common sizes being 12 to 14 inches. Some fish were as large as 16 inches, and one was a full 24 inches!

Flows
November to March flows average 20 to 50 cubic feet per second.

Access
Parking is plentiful, but even in winter the area gets crowded, so head out early.

Winter Strategy
With only 20 cubic feet per second coming from the dam in the winter, the size of the pool where most of the fish hold for the winter is drastically shrunk. Unfortunately, this is the closest open trout water to the north Front Range population center at this time of year, and as you might expect, crowds of anglers ascend to this spot regularly. Arrive early on a midweek day, and stake out a spot. You may have to hold it for a couple of hours before the fish get active.

PRO TIP

Estes Park becomes virtually devoid of tourists in the winter, so the hotel and motel rates can drop dramatically. The fly shops also drop their guide rates, some by as much as 25 percent. See Appendix E for shops in the area.

Tactics and Flies

A 9-foot 4W rod is perfect for fishing here. The hatches will be primarily midges, but the mayfly nymphs will be on the move, so some combination of these two insects in a 2-nymph setup will be most effective. Suggested flies are bead head Pheasant Tails #16 to #20, bead head Brassie #18 to #22 in olive, cream, or gray, Blue-Winged Olive Parachute #16 to #22 in various colors, and Midge Dry Flies #20 to #28.

NORTHWEST REGION

11. BLUE RIVER

The Blue River tailwater, one of the more popular winter fisheries in the state, comes out of the Dillon Reservoir and runs through the town of Silverthorne. Depending on the weather, 3 or 4 miles of water stay open all winter for fishing, but there's always at least a mile or so of open water through town.

Population
Very large, very wily rainbow trout, some as large as 10 pounds (and quite a few less picky fish in the 13- to 16-inch range) can be found there.

Flows
Winter flows average between 50 and 60 cubic feet per second, so in January and February the pools are going to hold a majority of the fish.

Access
The entire river through the town of Silverthorne is open to fishing, and many parking places are available. While the highway along the river is plowed regularly, only about the first 4 miles stays ice free in the coldest weather. And the river gets heavily fished, probably because of the easy access from I-70, as well as its reputation for big fish.

Winter Strategy
By January fish will be holding in the deepest holes. As with all winter fishing, you will need to find those pockets of water, taking your fly to the fish. In the colder water trout will not want to expend any unnecessary energy to feed. The fish are known to be shy of strike indicators and split shot, so using a high floating line such as a Rio Gold with a light-colored tip can take the place of a strike indicator. Using nymphs and larvae with dark-colored tungsten beads is also suggested. The fishing can be highly technical—these fish need to almost be hit in the nose to take a fly. Long, natural drifts are the way to go.

Corey Bolyard (right) and Willie Tiefel find that getting to the riverbank can be tough in the winter. Jon Spiegel

Tactics and Flies

Standard 9-foot 5W to 6W rods are fine for almost all fishing on the Blue River in the winter, and 6X to 7X tippet will be needed to fish midges size #22 and smaller and mysis shrimp patterns #18 to #22. Don't get hung up on specific patterns in winter fishing; concentrate on size and color. Always have an assortment of reds and blacks #22 to #26 or smaller. If you're unable to tell exactly what the midges look like, try a red or black Jujubee on those sunny days when fish will be looking for emerging bugs. Other worthwhile flies are the Poison Tung with a ⁵⁄₆₄ black tungsten bead head; red Brassies; Black Beauties; black, brown, or gray RS-2s; black Midges; Parachute Adams; and Griffin's Gnat.

12. WILLIAMS FORK RIVER BELOW WILLIAMS FORK RESERVOIR

A 2-mile fishery near the town of Parshall, the Williams Fork River tailwater begins at the dam below Williams Fork Reservoir and ends at the confluence with the Colorado River. The river features riffles, runs, and deep pools, with undercut banks in narrow spots. Given the prolific midge hatches (and the lack of angling competition), it's a good option for winter fishing.

The Willams Fork River below Williams Fork Reservoir is 2 miles of great winter fishing. RUSSELL MILLER

Population

The fishing is consistently good, with the average size of trout being about 14 inches.

Flows

January and February water flows will average between 65 and 75 cubic feet per second.

Access

To access the river turn south at Parshall on CR 3 for 1 mile to a parking area for river access. There's a hike of about a mile to the fishing, and it can get pretty cold and windy, so take a backpack with clothes, food, and warm drink.

Winter Strategy

Fish seem to stay in the deeper pools and out of the feeding lanes even when the temperature is in the low thirties, but they feed very aggressively. Around 12:30 p.m., you might get a few on the surface, but most of the action will be on the bottom. You may have to adjust your rig a couple of times to get down to where the fish are. Keep adding weight and adjusting your strike indicator until you can dredge the deep pools. If you have the proper weight and strike indicator position, the split shot should be bouncing on the bottom from time to time.

Tactics and Flies

This is not a big water like the nearby Colorado River, and a 9-foot 5W rod will do the trick. Use a red Copper John #18 with a black RS-2 #20 to #22 below. Other flies to try are WD-40s, Barr's Pure Midge Larva, Rojo, Jujubees, Disco Midges, Miracles, Befus Glass Bead Emergers, Midge Adams, and Brooks Sprout Midges, all in size #20 or smaller.

SOUTHEAST REGION

14. Arkansas River tailwater

Thanks to a multimillion-dollar stream improvement project, the Arkansas River below Pueblo Reservoir has become one of the more angler-friendly tailwater fisheries in the state, especially during the fall, winter, and early spring. In fact, it is an incredibly unique experience to be able to fish here in the winter—almost as if it were spring or fall. I don't know of another site like this. The air temperature in town combines with the water temperature in this low-elevation reservoir to create this environment. And since the normally free-flowing Arkansas River isn't fishable in winter—too cold and mostly covered with ice—it's great to be able to fish the tailwater. It can be reached by exiting Pueblo from I-25 onto US 50 West, turning south on Pueblo Boulevard, then heading west on Nature Center Road.

Population
Despite the lack of formal population surveys, this is hands down one of the best winter fishing experiences in the state: The water temperature from the reservoir allows insect hatches that would not otherwise occur in the winter. The water temperature in Pueblo averages about 10 degrees warmer than that in the Denver metro area and 30 to 50 degrees warmer than most other tailwaters. And while the water is whirling disease positive, it's also heavily stocked with rainbows that have grown larger than the size in which WD organisms can cause deformities. There is also a decent-size resident population of browns.

Flows
Flows remain stable between 70 and 150 cubic feet per second.

Access
A trail 8 miles long parallels the river through Pueblo. There are seven parking areas for anglers, including spots just below the dam. Standard regulations apply, but catch-and-release is strongly encouraged.

Winter Strategy
With stable fall and winter flows, this stretch fishes best between November and March. The highest trout numbers are in the 2-mile stretch starting at

The author caught this nice rainbow in February in the Arkansas River, just below Pueblo Reservoir dam. Otsie Stowell

the dam. The average fish in this section is between 9 and 14 inches long, with some as large as 15 to 18 inches. The lower sections (which mostly run through industrial and business areas, so the scenery is not so good) offer the best fishing. The fish are between 12 and 16 inches and have taken on all the characteristics of wild trout. The lower section is not stocked, but fish have migrated downstream.

The water will come up slowly through March, April, and May, and this requires fishing nymphs with heavier weights and bead head flies to get down to the fish. By April the river downstream through the town will begin producing some caddis. But the channel through town is narrower and is bordered by 8-foot-high concrete walls. Wading can become quite hazardous, even while the water below the dam stays fishable until about 450 c.f.s. Once the release from the reservoirs upstream hits, the river swells to 6,000 c.f.s. and will stay high (near 1,000 c.f.s.) until October. The flows can also change very quickly. Until that time enjoy summerlike fishing in unsummer-like weather, a truly remarkable situation. And be ready to start all over again in November.

Tactics and Flies

Anglers can expect hatches of midges, blue-winged olive mayflies, caddis, yellow Sally stoneflies, and pale morning dun and trico mayflies. Blue-winged olives hatch all winter, and midge hatches make December and January 2 good months of dry fly fishing. Several techniques are effective in fishing these tailwater trout. A standard 2-fly nymphing rig is used in the riffles, runs, and pocket water. Large #10 to #12 Prince Nymphs, crane fly imitations, and stoneflies on a tandem rig with #16 to #18 tungsten Pheasant Tails, Mighty Mite Baetis, Mercury Pheasant Tail RS-2s, Zebra Midges, Brassies, or Black Beauties, all in #18 to #20, are all effective.

Dry/dropper rigs are effective in the riffles. Use a #14 to #16 PMX, #12 to #16 Rubber-Legged Stimulator, #16 to #18 Goddard or Elkhair Caddis, or #14 to #16 Parachute Adams for a dry-fly indicator, and drop any small, flashy nymph below that. Trout rising in the flats can be spooky, so use a 12-foot leader. For most hatches use an appropriately sized Parachute Adams #18 and Sparkle Dun #18 to #20 in a 2-fly rig.

In fall/winter fishing streamers are often the best fly to hook larger trout in the lower river. A #6 to #12 bead head Woolly Bugger (olive and rust), a black Conehead Bugger, or Autumn Splendor are good starting choices in the fall and all winter long.

WINTER SEASON SUMMARY

Winter fly fishing may separate the fanatics from the "normal" anglers, but the challenge, solitude, and unique opportunities draw more and more anglers into the season every year. For those who have yet to try winter fishing, the Arkansas River in Pueblo is a good transition to determine if you are ready for the big time.

There are not a lot of tactical options in winter fishing. The real trick is to get the flies (some combination of midges) down to where the fish are so they don't have to work too hard. Do that, and you'll be successful. You can always try a streamer. That's what I caught the fish (in the photo) on below Pueblo Dam in February one year. And yes, we ate that one or I wouldn't have been holding it that way. Honestly, it didn't taste that good. It was probably a hatchery brood fish that had eaten trout kibble its entire life. But it sure gobbled my streamer.

SPRING

MARCH TO RUNOFF

Fishing in the springtime has a couple of things going for it: The fish are hungry, and their little fish brains are still half frozen. The problem is that fly fishers are being squeezed at the beginning, waiting for the water temps to hit 50 degrees and the blue-winged olive mayflies to start hatching, and on the other end for that wall of runoff water to come crashing down the river,

Spring weather in Colorado can be unpredictable. It's best to be prepared for almost anything. TIM ROMANO

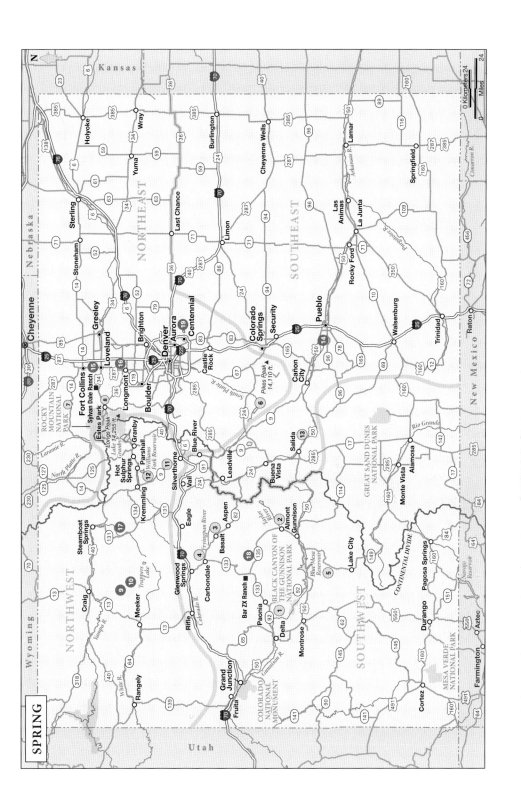

ruining the fishing for anywhere from 2 to 6 weeks. The weather doesn't cooperate all that well either. Rainstorms and snowstorms can turn the water off-color at any time before runoff begins.

When you finally do get out, it's often as though you are beginning all over. Your flies get hung up in the trees or on submerged branches or moss in the water. Your knots don't work well, and you get tangles in the line, especially on 2-fly rigs.

But you keep going out, and things fall into place. You haul in a nice rainbow or two, and you remember why you're doing it. You're in the groove.

SOUTHWEST REGION

1. Gunnison River in Gunnison Gorge

With an astounding average 7,000 brown trout per mile (see the Summer section for more information), the Gunnison Gorge is a tempting fishery, no matter the season. In the spring, however, the higher flows and cloudy water make it an intimidating prospect.

Population

A 2005 fish census estimated an astounding average 7,000 brown trout per mile throughout its 14-mile length. Many of those fish are in the 15- to 18-inch range. The largest were 24 to 27 inches long. There was a smattering of rainbows present, but by 2012 the stocking of Hofer whirling disease (WD)–resistant rainbows should bring those numbers up quite a bit.

Flows

On April 15, 2011, for instance, the Gunnison River in the Gorge was flowing 1,200 cubic feet per second. (The water releases started a little early that year.) At 500 c.f.s., for comparison, the water is considered too fast to wade safely.

Access

To get to Pleasure Park, which is well marked, drive about 12 miles east of Delta on CO 92. In the spring the North Fork will be too high to wade, but there will be boats you can hire to ferry you across. On the other side a 4-mile-long trail follows the northeast bank of the river. This is known as the Smith Fork trail. The bank is manageable on this side and allows greater access to the river. Anglers are encouraged to wear a wading belt, have a wading staff, and wear studded felt or rubber soles for safety anywhere on the river.

> **PRO TIP**
>
> There are three local float-trip guide services into the Gunnison Gorge. Fees are charged per person per day. Multiple-day trips are the norm, with camping along the river. All fishing and camping equipment and supplies are provided. See Appendix E for more information on Gunnison Gorge fly shops and guide services.

Another option is to take CO 92 east to Read and turn on H 75 Road, continuing east until South River Road forks to the right. Stay on that until you hit Cottonwood Campground. At that point you can continue south on the road as it parallels the river or stop and take the West River Trail south along the river.

Spring Strategy

I suggest that (especially) first-time anglers hire a float guide/outfitter to fish the Gunnison—in any season. A single float trip would be all you would need to return on your own. There are simply too many variables to have much chance of a successful fishing experience on a one-day trip into the gorge the first time out.

If you do decide to hike, take some comfort in the fact that the slower current in the rivers is near the banks and will be until runoff subsides, and that's where most of the fish will be holding. Look for any slick water to cast to because those will be the slowest spots.

All the water in the gorge is released from Crystal Reservoir by the Bureau of Reclamation. There's always an annual flood in May that quickly spikes at 4,000 c.f.s. This is done to simulate natural flows and thus restore the river to ecological health. The flow rates rise very quickly but then drop just as quickly to between 600 and 1,000 c.f.s.

Tactics and Flies

This is big water. A 9 or 9½-foot 6W to 7W rod is a good idea on this stretch because it extends your casting range by 10 to 15 feet and allows heavier flies or streamers to be used. A 4X leader will be sufficient for the big flies you'll need and a 3XS leader for the streamers. Set your indicator, weight, and flies up according to the Gale Doudy method described in the Gunnison Gorge fall section on page 68. Blue-winged olive mayflies and caddis will be the two major hatches before runoff strikes, with midges still hanging around. Stonefly nymphs are always a good top fly in any 2-fly rigs, with a BWO nymph or emerger or a green caddis larvae or emerger as a dropper. Try a Bitch Creek, a Half Back, or a Flash Prince #6 to #10 for the stonefly. These insects are in the water well before any hatching is evident and are kicked loose by the current. A 2-fly rig of an egg fly #12 to #16 and a red or orange San Juan Worm #12 to #16 will take fish. If you want to fish streamers, use a solid color with a little flash Conehead Woolly Bugger #2 to #6 and a full strip retrieve through the smooth spots.

2. TAYLOR RIVER

This section of the Taylor River begins below Taylor Park Reservoir in the upper Gunnison Basin and runs 20 miles southwest to join the East River at Almont, where they merge to become the Gunnison River. The upper 0.4 mile (a true four-season fishery) is a meadow river with huge trout, mostly rainbows.

Population
While I haven't seen any population surveys, the pounds-per-acre measure is probably the highest in the state. Creel-census surveys on the lower river are not particularly high, most likely the result of inexperienced anglers fishing at random spots along the river, then reporting few fish caught. If planning was ever necessary, it would be on the Taylor River, upper or lower section. This river is WD-positive.

Flows
From April until runoff the Taylor River flows at 100 to 125 cubic feet per second below the dam and about 200 c.f.s. at Almont. Both of these flows are easily wadable, but wading is discouraged in the tailwater pool. In the lower river where the flows are higher, just watch out for deeper pools.

Access
There are many places to park along the public access portion (11 miles) of the lower river and quite a few on the upper 0.4 mile. The problem is that snow and rock slides close this road upon occasion. The danger is not so much getting hit by a slide as it is being cut off from civilization. There are a few guest ranches in the upper canyon but they are often owned by multi-national corporations, which may or may not be friendly to locals. Wait until the snow is off the slopes and the ice is off the river and you should be alright. There will be plenty of parking space in the spring.

Spring Strategy
Rainbows are spring spawners, but because they are such a resource in the tailwater, anglers are asked not to disturb them on their spawning beds. If you can't wade there, you probably won't bother them, and it is difficult to tell a spawning trout from one that is just in the feeding lane. Spawners

don't move very much and rarely chase a bug in the water. What spawners will do is fan the area with their tail to remove sediment from around the eggs. If you can't tell, the best way to not disturb them is to avoid throwing a streamer into that area, because a spawner will attack to protect its eggs. If you do catch one and it's brightly colored, just get it back into the water quickly, because other fish will raid the redd (or spawning bed) to eat the eggs. That doesn't mean you shouldn't use egg flies. In fact, that's when you want to use them because fish are looking for eggs that have broken loose from the bed.

PRO TIP

If nothing else is working on the lower river, use a brown stonefly nymph size #4 to #6 and golden stonefly nymph size #10 to #12. Remember, stoneflies are active under the surface for three years before they hatch, and a big hatch will occur in a few weeks. A double stonefly rig like this is heavy, so proper placement of a strike indicator is key to making it work. The lower fly should nick the bottom.

On the lower river the blue-winged olive mayflies will be gearing up for a big hatch in May, but until then the action is still on midges. Stonefly nymphs are always in the water, and fish coming out of a tough winter will be looking for them. Look for some caddis as runoff begins.

Tactics and Flies

Fish don't move much in this cold water, so a natural drift is critical, and the hook should be set as soon as a fish in proximity to your flies moves or even opens its mouth. Set the hook by flipping the rod tip in a short arc downstream with the tip finishing just above the water. Flies on tailwaters should be a size smaller than you'd use on freestone rivers. Nymph/larvae patterns should be #18 to #24, and mysis shrimp patterns should be #18 to #22.

Other recommended tailwater flies are Jujubee Midge #20 to #22, Brassie #20 to #22, Black Beauty #20 to #24, red Disco Midge #18 to #22, and egg flies #14 to #18.

On the lower river the fish will start moving out of the deep holes as the water warms and into shallows and riffles for the BWO hatches. Use small mayfly nymphs #18 to #22, such as Pheasant Tails (regular and flashback) and Copper Johns in red, black, copper, and chartreuse. For stoneflies use a 20-Incher #6 to #10 or Rubber Leg Stonefly #6 and Juju Baetis #20, Jujubee

Midges #18 to #22, and Rojo Midges #20. Once the hatch arrives use a dry fly, such as a Parachute Adams, a Blue Quill, or a Parachute Dun #18 on top and trail a Barr's BWO Emerger #20.

Except for midges, most aquatic insects won't hatch in freestone streams until the water temperature reaches about 50 degrees. Midges can hatch when the water temperature is near freezing, if the other conditions are favorable. Among the most common of these conditions is a quick (if slight) warming of the water, such as is produced by a period of sunlight or a rapid increase of the air temperature. In the tailwater, where the water temperature rarely if ever reaches 50 degrees, the insects have adapted to the colder temperatures and hatch in lower temperatures and are also smaller than their freewater counterparts.

3. Fryingpan River

This stretch of the Fryingpan River begins at Ruedi Reservoir dam and ends at its confluence with the Roaring Fork River at the town of Basalt. Most of the river should be open and fishable in spring. Sunlight will bring fish out of their holes for better goodies to eat.

Population

A 2010 population survey at the Baetis Bridge (the first bridge below the dam) estimated 1,114 brown trout and 425 rainbow trout per acre at that survey site, with 525 browns and 134 rainbows larger than 14 inches per mile in the same area. Hofer strain rainbows have been stocked in the Fryingpan for 4 years.

An area called the Toilet Bowl, just below the dam, holds trout in the 10- to 15-pound range. The presence of mysis shrimp from the reservoir explains the size of these fish. The upper 2 miles has catch-and-release, fly-and-lure-only restrictions.

Flows

To show you how unpredictable the water flows can be, May 2010 saw the water running at 125 cubic feet per second. A year later in the same month, it is so far averaging 345 c.f.s. In 2011 Colorado has had nearly record snow-falls in some watersheds, so the higher flows are an attempt to empty the reservoir before the snowmelt fills it. The water gods in Colorado like to control the releases for maximum benefit. Spilling reservoirs mean water is going to end up free in Arizona and California, and free is bad, to their thinking. But the only thing you need to worry about is whether you will be wade-fishing the pools or fishing the slow water along the banks.

Access

Many anglers fish the upper mile, given its easy access and parking, but the fish populations in the second mile are only a little less than the upper mile, and fewer anglers are on that water. Access to the lower river is plentiful, with more than 8 miles open to the public between the town of Basalt and the 2 miles of catch-and-release water below the dam. There is usually parking adjacent to the public water in the lower stretch, but if you get there late, it may require some hiking.

Jon Spiegel shows a good-size spring rainbow from the Fryingpan River. With the water low and clear, be on the lookout for paired-up fish. They could be mating and shouldn't be bothered. RUSSELL MILLER

Spring Strategy

In normal years water will be warming slightly and the flows rising slowly until the aforementioned scheduled water dump. Fish will be moving out of their winter holding spots and moving to slow water along the edges of the river and pocket water created by rocks and debris in the river. Blue-winged olive mayflies and midges will be hatching beginning in late morning and heat up until 3 p.m. These hatch times won't change much until after the high water recedes, but the midges will be less important and the BWOs will be more important as runoff nears.

In 2010 the peak flow reached 800 c.f.s. and fell quickly. Needless to say, it varies widely year to year.

The pool just below the dam is where the huge fish stay fat on mysis shrimp. There are also high numbers of Hofer strain rainbows just below the dam, which reached the 20-inch range in 2011. These and the perennial residents of the Toilet Bowl will still be eating mysis shrimp and getting bigger until the big flows hit.

Tactics and Flies

When fishing nymphs, larvae, and emergers, tippets should be 6X and 7X for dry flies. The midges at this time of the year come in all sizes, from the winter midges #16 to microscopic at #32. For sanity's sake ignore the smallest midges, and stick with patterns between #16 and #24.

By May the blue-winged olive mayfly, #16 to #24, is coming off. All life stages are important to the angler at this time. The nymphs tend to be dark, #18 to #20, and black or dark olive patterns work best. Various emerger patterns, #18 to #22, as well as nymphs, can be floated in surface film effectively or weighted for the lower or middle water column. Adults, such as the Blue Dun or Blue Quill or parachute styles #16 to #24, can be effective. It's important to capture the insects to estimate size and coloration of the predominant type coming off.

Dry flies, such as Matt's Midge #18 to #20, Griffin's Gnat #16 to #22, and Sprout Midge #16 to #20, are effective when trout rise to the surface and show their mouths. Effective dry BWO patterns are Parachute Quill Body BWO, Sparkle Dun BWO, Parachute Emerger BWO, and No-Hackle BWO, all in #16 to #22.

In low-light situations, try small streamers, such as black, brown, and olive Woolly Buggers tied with a little flash #10 to #12.

Small Epoxyback Golden Stonefly Nymphs or black stonefly nymphs #10 to #16, such as K's Stonefly, work well for the top fly.

4. Roaring Fork River

The Roaring Fork River, given that its headwaters are high in the Hunter-Fryingpan Wilderness, is perhaps inordinately affected by spring runoff, particularly when compared to various tailwater fisheries.

Population

A recent fish stream census estimated that, in a 2.5-mile stretch of the Roaring Fork River below the town of Basalt, there were 2,300 brown trout and 3,000 whitefish. As of the late 1990s, whirling disease had all but wiped out the rainbow trout population in that reach. But this stretch of river is decent rainbow habitat, and with the stocking of the Hofer variety (WD-resistant) rainbows well under way, there should be a resurgence of the rainbow population in a short time.

Flows

April flows in the Roaring Fork are only around 200 cubic feet per second at Basalt, but with runoff they hit 1,400 c.f.s. by mid-May. Flows at Glenwood Springs are 800 c.f.s. in April but reach 3,000 c.f.s. by mid-May.

Access

Crowding will begin to be a problem in the spring but not a major one.

Spring Strategy

With a big, complex river like the Roaring Fork, planning a fishing trip is a little like working a jigsaw puzzle, a situation made more complex by the varying flows of spring runoff. Before leaving be sure to check with a local fly shop for updates as to the conditions.

The blue-winged olive mayfly hatch will begin in the lower river in late March and work its way upriver through April and May until runoff.

High, warming water will bring fish out of their deep pools and spread them into slow spots near the shore. The stoneflies will be moving around and should be fished in fast water with nymphs. Look for the blue-winged olive mayflies in the flat water in the afternoons. Egg patterns are worthwhile as the rainbows are spawning. Visibility will vary, so use patterns with a little flash for off-color water.

Tactics and Flies

In the river between Basalt and Carbondale, the fish will be sitting in slow water, lethargically feeding on midges and blue-winged olive nymphs but moving to riffle areas for midge hatches in the afternoon. Warm overcast days are best.

Use a double nymph rig with a weighted stonefly nymph (something like a 20-Incher or a Poxyback Golden) and a midge larvae or emerger (a black, brown, or gray RS-2). In March and early April, the fish will still hold in the deep pools at times but increasingly will start moving around as the water warms and rises. Fish the stoneflies in fast water with a BWO emerger #16 to #18. In the smooth water stick to small flies, such as a midge dry fly #18 to #22 and a BWO emerger.

Below Carbondale use the same flies but step the size of the stonefly up a notch or two. Egg flies such as the Flashtail Mini Egg #16 can be substituted for the midge. A Flash Prince or Tung Prince #12 can be substituted for the stonefly.

5. Lake Fork of the Gunnison River

Draining the northeastern section of the San Juan Mountains, the Lake Fork of the Gunnison River flows north through canyons and steep valleys in the upper section into Lake San Cristobal, through Lake City, and north through ranch country into Blue Mesa Reservoir.

Population

Brown trout make up about 80 percent of the fish sampled, rainbows the other 20 percent. The sampling estimated that there are 23 browns and 4 rainbows longer than 14 inches per surface acre of water. I've caught an 18-inch brownie adjacent to the Gate Campground and saw a 24-inch brown caught under the bridge just upstream from there. So there are big fish in this river if the angler is patient.

Because of whirling disease, rainbow trout reproduction declined from 1998 to 2008, but the Hofer strain of WD-resistant rainbows has been stocked since 2009. Expect better rainbow fishing in the coming years.

Flows

Stream flow is not measurable in the winter or spring because the water is frozen. By the time it's measurable in May, it is usually about 75 cubic feet per second.

Access

Most of the action is on the lower river, with a short stretch above the Gate Campground. A 5-mile stretch below the Gates (which are two very prominent vertical geologic structures) is private and marked by a steel cable stretched across the river at the upper boundary of the private property. Below the stretch that occurs when CO 149 comes off a long hill and turns south, CR 25 turns north, and public access begins about ¼ mile north. This is the beginning of the habitat-improved area.

> **PRO TIP**
>
> The habitat-improved area that begins about a half mile from the turnoff of CO 149 onto CR 25 is not well marked, and parking is mostly on the shoulder. About a half mile farther is a parking spot on the right that will hold several cars. Right below the parking area is a V-shaped water bar. Upstream from there is open to sunlight, and any insect activity on the Lake Fork will be happening there.

From that point downstream to Blue Mesa Reservoir all is public access. The river before Blue Mesa Reservoir is a narrow canyon with cascades and large pools and many places to park.

Spring Strategy

The river is ice covered until late March and clears in patches, given its north/south orientation and intermittent, steep canyon walls. Runoff will increase and drop erratically until early May when it shoots up, peaking around June 1 at 1,500 to 2,000 cubic feet per second.

The erratic nature of ice-off followed by early runoff makes creating a strategy for the spring a little difficult, according to Oscar Marks of the Gunnison River Fly Shop. Use a stonefly nymph or a double nymph rig with a large stonefly on top and a smaller yellow or black stonefly nymph as a dropper. These should be fished through riffle areas or runs at the end of a riffle. Blue-winged olive mayflies will begin hatching before runoff, and some caddis will also show up, but the real action is on stoneflies, Marks says.

Tactics and Flies

A 9-foot 5W rod will be sufficient for fishing most situations on the lake at this low-water stage. Depending upon air temperature, this fish could still be wintering in holes, moving around, or waiting until the sunlight to move into the riffles and pool edges to dine on BWOs. Multiply your chances with a double nymph rig with a small golden stone on top and a BWO nymph #18 or a chartreuse Copper John #18 to #20 as a trailer. If the fish are eating on top, put a BWO dry fly, such as a Parachute Adams on top and a Barr's BWO Emerger, nonweighted, as a trailer. A nonweighted trailer will keep your dry fly on top longer.

NORTHEAST REGION

6. SOUTH PLATTE RIVER IN ELEVEN MILE CANYON

This stretch of the South Platte River runs through a scenic canyon below the dam on Eleven Mile Reservoir and ends near Lake George on US 24, about 38 miles west of Colorado Springs. The canyon can be reached by turning south on Eleven Mile Canyon Road in Lake George and driving a mile. The river features long, slow meanders; riffle/run/pool complexes; and deep, lakelike pools and cascades.

Population

The catch-and-release section, stretching about 2 miles downstream from the dam, has one of the heaviest concentrations of rainbow trout in the entire state—more than 3,500 trout per mile. Most will be in the 12- to 14-inch range. They are so healthy that they seem much bigger when you are trying to land one. Surprisingly, rainbows are now populating the lower, nonrestricted 8 miles of river—something of a miracle, given that the entire South Platte River system has been hit hard by whirling disease. In the past 20 years, almost no rainbows have reproduced successfully in the entire river system—except in Eleven Mile Canyon.

Unfortunately, New Zealand mud snails have shown up at the fishery. These invaders can destroy a fishing site because they reproduce easily and quickly and they eat the same microorganisms as insects, decimating the fishes' food source. Boots and waders must be cleaned to keep the snails from spreading.

Flows

The average spring flow is 75 to 110 cubic feet per second. The ice starts receding in February and is mostly gone by late March.

Access

Access the river along the road in the lower 8 miles of river from parking lots and pull-offs on the road. In the upper 2 miles, parking is at a premium, so arrive early or plan on a hike. It's a good idea to get there early anyway, because fishing guides will get there early and camp on the best sections of

The author fights a decent rainbow in Eleven Mile Canyon just after ice-off. Midges are still very important at this time of the year, and this fish was taken on a large midge emerger. NANCY MORRELL

the river for the whole day. It's bad etiquette to move into an occupied spot, but the river is wide enough in many places that the far bank can be fished without interfering with anyone.

Spring Strategy

Midges will still be a mainstay in March and April, with the oversized winter midge (or snow midge, depending upon whom you talk to) leading the pack. By April, maybe as soon as late March, the blue-winged olive mayflies will begin to hatch. By the beginning of May, yellow Sally stoneflies will start to hatch. Just before the spring releases from the dam, some caddis will start hatching in the afternoon and evening. During high flows worms and scuds will be swept downstream. Fish treat these high protein morsels like stoneflies and gobble them up. And of course, egg patterns are always worth trying in Eleven Mile Canyon because the rainbows are spawning, and both rainbows and browns slurp eggs. It's a virtual slumgullion of bugs in and on the water. So don't lock into one bug or one pattern.

Tactics and Flies

A 9-foot 5W is plenty of rod for this stretch of river, but the 5X tippet will have to be stepped down to 6X on dropper midge larvae or BWO nymphs.

Parachute Adams #26, Matt's Midge #24, and Griffin's Gnat #24 are the dry flies of choice early in the spring. When nothing is hatching, use midge larvae #24 to #26 to sight-fish in slow, deep pools with a stonefly nymph on top. Poxy Golden Stones Nymphs #14 to #16 should be used when the Sallies are coming off. Drop one behind a #16 yellow Stimulator to double your action. Then use a Parachute Adams or a Parawulff BWO top fly with a Pheasant Tail nymph as a trailer, both #18 to #20, when the BWOs are moving.

7. CACHE LA POUDRE RIVER

The Cache La Poudre River canyon begins 10 miles northwest of Fort Collins and about a mile west of US 287 on CO 14. The river itself begins in Rocky Mountain National Park and runs 70 miles before reaching the flatlands and private property. Throughout its length there is everything from waterfalls and rapids to meadowlike, meandering stream cuts.

Population

Recent fish census surveys indicate that the highest population of fish—10 to 14 inches—were found in the Indian Meadows stretch.

The river's rainbow population was decimated by whirling disease in the 1990s. And while brown trout have largely filled many of the habitat niches historically occupied by rainbows, given the new strain of WD-resistant rainbows, this picture should change.

Flows

The average stream flow in the spring starts low (30 to 40 cubic feet per second or even lower), then gradually increases until runoff hits. During runoff the flows can double or triple overnight. In 2011 the entire river that parallels the highway was ice free by the first week in April. In some years the upper stretches will be ice covered for weeks longer.

Access

Wading access is extensive, but many pullouts are small, holding one to two vehicles. Most campgrounds, picnicking sites, and boat put-ins have parking spots designated for anglers. There is some private property far up the canyon where both banks are off limits, but it's nothing to worry about and is well marked. Bank ice will remain on much of the upper river until after the water itself becomes ice free. Be careful of the bank ice, as it is often unstable and dangerous to stand on.

Spring Strategy

Even if the river itself is ice free, the water temperature will often remain low enough at the higher elevations to keep fish immobile and discourage every insect hatch except for midges.

With low water and cold temperatures, the fish are going to be concentrated in deeper holes until the air temperature warms and encourages the midges. On warm, sunny days, the fish will move to the riffles to feed on hatching midges.

In most years the lower few miles of river at the mouth of the canyon will remain ice free. The BWOs will start hatching there in early April and move until runoff blows out the hatches. Stoneflies will begin their early molting stages and will be vulnerable to fish. Browns will take streamers, so if nothing else is working, use those.

Tactics and Flies

For BWO and midge hatches, use the Extended Body BWO #18 to #22; Film Critic BWO #18; Split Flag BWO #18; Eric's High-Vis Midge, or Biot Midge, both #20 to #22.

For nymphs and emergers try the Juju Midge #18 to #22 (all colors), Greg's Emerger #18 to #20, Juju Baetis #18 to #22, RS-2 #20 to #24, Pat's Rubber Legs Orange #8 to #10 (for stoneflies), Hot Wire Prince #16 to #18, IED #14, and orange and peach Micro Eggs #20.

8. Big Thompson River below Estes Park

This section of the Big Thompson River begins below Lake Estes in Estes Park and winds 20 miles down a canyon into the city of Loveland.

Population
Despite the presence of whirling disease, the Big Thompson is one of only two rivers in the state to have a healthy reproducing rainbow trout population. A trout population survey in a 572-foot section of the Big Thompson below Olympus Dam in 2009 estimated there were 149 rainbows and 112 brown trout larger than 6 inches, with the most common sizes being 12 to 14 inches. Some fish were as large as 16 inches.

Flows
Stream flow increases from 50 cubic feet per second in March to 400 c.f.s at runoff.

Access
Parking is not a problem here in the spring.

Spring Strategy
As the flows increase and the water warms, the fish will feel secure enough to move out of the deep holes and feed, and there will be more to feed on with the warmer temperature spurring hatches.

Blue-winged olive mayflies will begin to hatch in mid- to late April, especially on overcast days as the temperature warms. Stoneflies are ever present in the water a few miles below the dam and downstream. Both golden and dark stoneflies are found in relatively small sizes. Since rainbows will be spawning, egg patterns can land a hungry fish or two.

Tactics and Flies
A 9-foot 4W or 5W rod is perfect for fishing here.

The hatches will primarily be midges, but the mayfly nymphs will be on the move, so some combination of these two insects in a 2-nymph setup will be most effective. Suggested nymphs are bead head Pheasant Tails #16 to #20 and bead head Brassie #18 to #22 in olive, cream or gray. Blue-Winged Olive

Parachutes #16 to #22 in various colors and Midge Dry Flies #20 to #28 are effective topwater patterns.

Other dry fly patterns include Sprout Midges #20 to #24, CDC BWOs #18 to #22, Sprout BWOs #18 to #22, and Extended Body BWOs #20 to #22. Other effective nymph patterns are the Poison Tung #18 to #20, Desert Storm #20 to #22, Soft-Hackle Emergers #18 to #20, Juju Baetis #18 to #22, Flash Prince Nymphs (for stoneflies) #16 to #18, 20-Inchers #14 to #18, red Sparkle Worms #16 to #18, and Micro Eggs #18 to #20 in pink and orange.

For streamers use Tung Thin Mint #6 to #10 and Vanilla Buggers #6 to #8.

NORTHWEST REGION

11. BLUE RIVER

The Blue River tailwater, one of the more popular four-season fisheries in the state, comes out of Dillon Reservoir and through the town of Silverthorne.

Population
The Blue River from the Dillon dam downstream to Green Mountain Reservoir is rated as a Gold Medal Water, meaning the area has a high potential for trophy trout. All are fly and lure only, with immediate release of the fish. No fish survey results are available from the Colorado Division of Wildlife, but the DOW began stocking whirling disease–resistant Hofer strains of rainbows in 2009, so fishing success on the river below Dillon Reservoir should be on the rise.

Flows
Spring flows average between 50 and 200 cubic feet per second until heavy water releases hit in early June.

Access
There is excellent access on the river above Dillon Reservoir, by the tailwater section, and downstream to Green Mountain Reservoir and below. The access points are usually near habitat improvements or generally fine stretches of fishing water. The first access is the Blue River Campground, which is 6 miles from Silverthorne. Sutton Unit State Wildlife Area is 7 miles from town, Eagle's Nest Wildlife Area is 9 miles, and the Blue River Wildlife Area 17 miles. Most of the river above Dillon Reservoir and adjacent to Breckenridge is along the highway and has a bike/pedestrian path. Private property is clearly marked.

Spring Strategy
Fishing the Blue in the early spring is not much different from winter fishing. By May in most years, the ice will be gone from the entire stretch between Dillon Reservoir and Green Mountain Reservoir.

In the tailwater the fish are known to be shy of strike indicators and split shot, so using a high floating line with a light-colored tip, such as a

Some of the best fishing in the Blue River in spring is downstream from Silverthorne. TIM ROMANO

Rio Gold, can take the place of a strike indicator. Using nymphs and lar-vae with dark-colored tungsten beads is also suggested. These fish need to be hit in the nose or nearly so to take a fly. Long, natural drifts are the way to go. Rainbows are spawning in the Blue River by mid-April, so egg/midge tandems are effective, as are mysis/midge tandems in the river inside the town of Silverthorne. Try to avoid the spawning beds, and don't fish to spawning trout. The fishing in the river downstream from Green Mountain Reservoir can be a little off in the spring. Feeder streams' melt-off can discolor the water. Use a little flash and color in those conditions.

A double whammy tells you something about fishing the Blue River in the spring.
RUSSELL MILLER

Tactics and Flies

Standard 9-foot 5W to 6W rods are fine for almost all fishing on the Blue River, and 6X to 7X tippet will be needed to fish midges size #22 and smaller and mysis shrimp patterns #18 to #22. Recommended flies for spring are Mercury Midge #20 to #24, Dorsey's Mysis #22 to #24, Blood Midge #22 to #26, Black Beauty #22 to #24, Mercury Black Beauty #22 to #24, Mercury Pheasant Tail #20 to #24, red and black Mike's Midge #22 to #26, RS-2 #20 to #22, Jujubee Midge #22 to #24, Poison Tung Midge #20 to #22, Barr's Emerger #18 to #24, Juju Baetis #18 to #24, and Parachute Adams #18 to #24.

12. WILLIAMS FORK RIVER BELOW
WILLIAMS FORK RESERVOIR

The Williams Fork River tailwater is a 2-mile section of river near the town of Parshall on US 40. Check flows with local fly shops. No flow, no go.

Population

While the number of brown trout have generally declined in the Colorado River, angler reports have consistently reported good fishing on the Williams Fork tailwater. The average size of fish caught has been about 14 inches. Rainbow trout represent less than 1 percent of fish sampled or caught.

Flows

If there is a decent flow of 50 c.f.s. or higher, the fishing can be good but still unpredictable. Fishing at lower flows in the spring should be avoided to protect spawning rainbows.

Photographer Russell Miller displays the joy of spring—rainbow trout fishing.
JESSIE WYARD

Access

Access to the river can be gained by turning south at Parshall on CR 3 for 1 mile to a parking area for river access. The hike is about a mile. It can get pretty cold and windy in the spring, so take a backpack with clothes, food, and drink to stay comfortable.

Spring Strategy

Fishing in the spring can be problematic because of minimal flows, which may be true until water is released for downstream use or the water overflows the reservoir. Call a fly shop in the area before going. If the flows are minimal, the fish will be very spooky.

Tactics and Flies

This is not a big water like the nearby Colorado River, and a 9-foot 5W rod will do the trick. Use a red Copper John #18 with a black RS-2 #20 to #22 below. Other flies to try are WD-40s, Barr's Pure Midge Larva, Rojo Midges, Jujubee Midges, Disco Midges, Miracle Midges, Befus Glass Bead Emergers, Midge Adams, and Brooks Sprout Midges, all in size #20 or smaller. "Spring" or "snow" midges might hatch if the flow comes up. If so, use a gray RS-2 #16.

SOUTHEAST REGION

13. ARKANSAS RIVER

The Arkansas River is born along the slopes of Colorado's Collegiate Peaks, southwest of Leadville. There are 150 miles of free-flowing brown trout water before it pours into the plains east of the city of Pueblo. It flows through miles of meadow water and wild canyons, offering something for everybody along its stretches in the mountains. Almost all is open to floating, but only about 75 miles is open to foot access, more than enough for a lifetime of fishing.

The Arkansas River is a river of superlatives. The size and diversity of the water makes it very difficult to fish. But like most other fisheries in the spring, it starts off like a pussycat and ends up like a tiger. The flows are increasing, and honestly, there are only two hatches of note to consider. But they are both world class and turn the river into a churning vat of fish, at least for a few days.

Population

It's difficult to survey a river the size of the Arkansas, but there are many stretches with incredible numbers of brown trout. One thing everybody agrees upon is that it's a river on its way up, particularly since a ban on mine tailings has reduced pollution. Estimates indicate there are as many as 4,000 brown trout per mile in many stretches of the river between Salida and Cañon City. Above Salida there are still plenty of fish, but possibly not as many because of the fast current in the canyons.

Flows

Water flows in the spring vary between 100 and 150 cubic feet per second above Buena Vista from mid-March to mid-April and from 400 to 600 c.f.s. in Cañon City for that same period. By June 30 the flow rate is between 400 and 1,000 c.f.s. above Buena Vista and from 1,000 to 4,500 c.f.s. at Cañon City.

Access

The Arkansas is managed by a consortium of local, state, and federal agencies called the Arkansas Headwaters Recreation Association. This group has produced a detailed and accurate map of the river and public access areas.

It is given away locally along the river and by the Arkansas Headwaters Recreation Area at 307 West Sackett, Salida, CO 81201.

Spring Strategy

Fishing in the spring can be rainy, snowy, cold, and blustery. And when the caddis hatch is on (April 15 to May 15), most motels will be booked, parking areas full, and the fly shops packed, and long lines will form in restaurants. It's an excellent idea to plan ahead.

The blue-winged olive mayfly hatch begins in Cañon City around April 1 and works its way upstream to Leadville by May, hatching when the water temperature hits 50 degrees or thereabouts. The second hatch, of *Brachycentrus caddis,* begins in Cañon City about April 15 and lasts until runoff blows out the hatch. The caddis hatch typically makes it all the way to near Buena Vista before runoff. It's hard to describe these hatches, but the caddis are so thick that cars have to turn on windshield wipers to clear them off their windshields. Anglers wear breathing and sight protection to keep the bugs out of eyes, ears, nose, and throat. These two hatches are the best chance an angler has to catch some of the really big browns that are found in the Arkansas—the fish that normally feed at night, according to Bill Edrington, owner of Royal Gorge Anglers, in Cañon City.

> ### PRO TIP
>
> The wading angler needs to be here any time from April 1 to May 15 for the BWO hatch and then for the "mutha" of them all, the *Brachycentrus caddis* hatch from April 15 to about May 15.

There's also the problem of getting the fish to notice your fly when several thousand bugs are launching from the same area. If this is the case, Edrington suggests driving a couple of miles upriver from a hatch and fishing caddis larvae or pupa emergers. After all, the most action is below the water, and fish don't like to waste energy—until they go loco at all the bugs available.

Tactics and Flies

For equipment, a 9-foot 5W rod will cover most situations on this river in the early spring. If you are planning on throwing some heavy nymphs or streamers, a fast-action 9 to 9½-foot 6W rod might be preferable. Edrington says the Arkansas brown trout will just as likely take attractor flies as anything

An angler gets some early spring action on the Arkansas River beneath the Collegiate Peaks. RUSSELL MILLER

more visually accurate—flies such as the Yellow Humpy, Royal Wulff, Renegade, and Royal Coachman Trude on top and nymphs such as Pheasant Tails, Hare's Ears, and Prince Nymphs as the dropper flies—so if all the hatch information gets too confusing, just try these time-tested attractor patterns.

It's also worth trying a golden stonefly pattern on top and a BWO emerger such as the WD-40 or RS-2 #16 to #20 as the dropper. These patterns work as well for midge emergers and the BWOs, and the midges in the Arkansas are not the micro-teensie bugs you find in most Colorado rivers.

The hatches are early in the day, and the BWOs lay their eggs in the afternoons when the weather is warmest. With quite a bit of flat water still around, this is prime dry-fly time. Put a standard Parachute Adams or a Parawulff BWO, both in sizes #16 to #20, as your top fly and a bead head Pheasant Tail nymph #16 to #20 or an olive bead head Hare's Ear #16 to #20 as your dropper.

SPRING SEASON SUMMARY

My recommendation? Fish the Arkansas River just ahead of the hatch. Use a 2-fly setup, with a caddis emerger on top and a larvae below, or a golden stonefly nymph and a caddis emerger as the dropper. The top caddis fly should be a Banksia Bug #14 and a green Barr's Net Builder caddis larvae. For the second suggestion use a Poxyback Golden Stone #12 and a Banksia Bug #14. I would also recommend trying the Fryingpan River, using any of the flies just mentioned.

RUNOFF

While it's true that runoff tends to shut down most trout fishing for a period of time each year (especially during the peak water flows), there are other options for devoted Colorado fly fishers.

Take carp, for instance. There have been books written about fly fishing for this most unattractive yet underappreciated of coarse fish. Carp fight like the dickens, especially in light of the fact that some grow to 48 inches or larger. But if carp aren't to your taste, many lowland lakes teem with bluegills, perch, and crappy, all of which make for a great Saturday afternoon spent fishing with poppers. Especially if you're teaching a youngster to fly fish, this can be a rewarding way to spend a day in May or June.

But there are also places to fly fish for trout during runoff. And while it's often going to cost you a decent chunk of money (that's the bad news), the good news is that you can get into some of the biggest fish of the year and not have to worry about nitpicky stuff such as equipment, tactics, or fly selection. These trips usually require guides, and that's what guides do—take care of the nitpicky stuff.

Besides the guide fees (charges are per person per day), some of these places also have daily rod fees, which go directly to the landowners. If you can afford it, it sure beats sitting at home tying up yet another Woolly Bugger.

For convenience I have included fisheries on the West Slope, in central Colorado, and on the Front Range. And you won't have to look at carp.

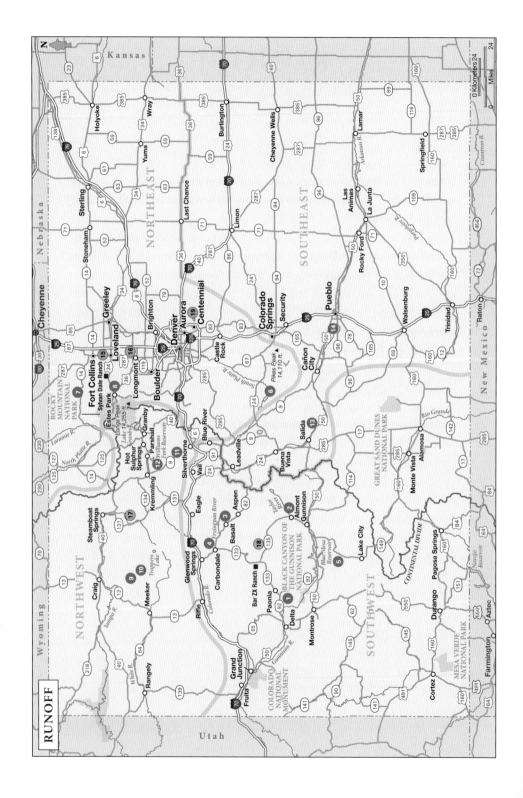

15. Sylvan Dale Ranch (Front Range)

This 3,200-acre, incredibly popular guest ranch is located just east of Big Thompson Canyon on US 34, about 5 miles west of Loveland. There are several lakes on the property, including Island Lake, which has rainbows, and Big Lake, which has largemouth and smallmouth bass. Weldon Spring Lake and Long Lake feature big rainbows (up to 20 inches). Big Valley Lakes is limited to fly fishing with barbless hooks only and immediate release of fish. The fish here are even larger than those in Weldon Spring and Long Lakes.

Some catch-and-keep fishing is allowed on a limited, supervised basis.

A guide is required on the first trip for one or two anglers at a cost of several hundred dollars per person. On following days anglers who are guests at the ranch can fish unguided for considerably less. Individual day visitors must always have a guide present at the higher rate. Lists of guides are supplied by the ranch. Equipment rentals (rods, waders, float tubes) are available. The Big Thompson River flows through the property, so depending on runoff, you can fish the river with improved habitat and stocked browns and rainbows.

The resort is a hopping place (hosting weddings, conferences, and vacationers and offering mountain biking, hayrides, trail riding, riding lessons, and cattle drives), but the lakes are semi-isolated. And as mentioned above, guests get reduced rates on fishing. The approval rate by guests for their stays is very good, especially for families with children.

For more information see www.sylvandale.com, or call (970) 667-3915.

16. St. Vrain State Park Ponds

For a low-cost Front Range alternative, try St. Vrain State Park on I-25. It's about 24 miles north of Denver and 7 miles east of Longmont on CO 119. Annually, 40,000 10-inch rainbow trout are stocked (20,000 in the spring and 20,000 in the fall), primarily in three of the seven ponds—Sandpiper, Mallard, and Coot ponds. The park encompasses more than 600 acres and features ponds, hiking trails, and campgrounds with full facilities.

Though located in a semirural area, the campground remains busy and crowded at times, but ice comes off the water in April or May, and all types of fishing are allowed: flies, lures, and bait, with standard bag and possession limits. Float tubes are highly recommended. It's a great place to work out the kinks before the summer season starts and very accessible for children who want to fish from the banks. The average size of fish is 10 to 12 inches.

For more information call (303) 678-9402 or go to www.parks.state.co.us.

17. Bull Basin Ranch, Antero and Spinney Reservoirs

Bull Basin Ranch is located in the Troublesome Creek watershed, north of Kremmling on US 40, between Steamboat Springs and Granby. The properties feature three Stillwater fisheries—Hidden Valley Lake, Black Mountain Pond, and Grandma's Pond.

Hidden Valley Lake is in the high desert, nested among the sagebrush. It is spring fed and as such has more biomass (scuds, leeches, water boatmen, *Callibaetis,* and damselfly hatches) than most Colorado waters, with

A deceptively small stream, Troublesome Creek can produce unexpectedly large fish. Dean Billington / Bull Basin Outfitters

Two anglers fish the quiet spring waters of Slate Mountain Creek on Bull Basin Ranch. Given the spring-fed streams and lakes, some of the Bull Basin waters can be fished during winter as well as during runoff. Dean Billington / Bull Basin Outfitters

the year-round, constant water temperature acting like a spring creek. Rainbows are the main fish species, but browns, cutthroat, and brookies are also present. The rainbows often reach 26 inches and the brookies 20 inches.

Black Mountain Pond is another spring-fed lake, but one loaded with freshwater shrimp. If you've read any of this book, you'll know what this means: really big fish. The pond is stocked with rainbow, brown, cutthroat, cutbow, and brook trout, and the fish average between 3 and 5 pounds, with some in double digits and "some too big to land."

Grandma's Pond is described as a "great little pond full of fat brookies and rainbows." It's great for all anglers but especially for beginners. "The trout are always willing to cooperate."

When the runoff is manageable, anglers enjoy Troublesome Creek, with several miles of habitat-improved stream through Bull Basin property. Featuring a great variety of stream habitat, the creek is home to rainbows, brownies, brookies, cuttbows and cutthroats, averaging 16 to 20 inches, with some up to 10 pounds.

Bull Basin Outfitters is the primary access to the ranch. See www.bullba sin.com or contact info@ bullbasin.com for more information.

Cutthroat Anglers in Silverthorne offers half-day trips and full-day floats on Antero and Spinney Mountain Reservoirs in South Park. Most property owners and outfitters limit the number of anglers to ensure a quality fishing experience. That is true of the Bull Basin properties but Spinney and Antero are public waters. While they don't limit numbers of fishermen, the lakes are closed until certain dates, which vary depending upon the severity of the winter—usually mid May. Both lakes are relatively shallow, highly productive water and grow fish 18 inches and larger. Of course, they are open to the public and can be fished from the bank, a float tube, or a nonmotorized boat. The advantage to using a guide is that they can put you onto fish the first time out, while the learning curve is fairly steep for the untutored. After the guides show you how to do it, you can return and rightly expect a certain amount of success for free.

See the Cutthroat Anglers website, www.fishcolorado.com, e-mail them at anglers@fishcolorado.com, or call (970) 262-2878.

18. Bar ZX Ranch

The Bar ZX Ranch is located near Paonia and offers world-class fishing. There are 29 lakes on the ranch, and each one is stocked with predominantly one type of trout from around the globe. One is full of Montana brook trout, another has large Snake River cutthroats, another tiger trout, and still another has Tasmanian rainbows (New Zealand).

Most of the ice will be off the lakes by runoff, and some are spring fed, which means they are ice free most of the year. And just after ice-out is the time trout are most active because they've basically been underfed for about 6 months.

Call Taylor Creek Fly Shops at (970) 927-4374 for more information, or e-mail the shop at tcreek@ssv.net for fees. The prices are comparable with those at Bull Basin.

19. Aurora Reservoir

Aurora Reservoir is an 820-acre impoundment in the Denver suburb of Aurora. To get there take the South Parker Road exit on I-225, and drive 1.75 miles to Quincy Avenue. Proceed east for 6 miles to the reservoir.

The reservoir is stocked annually with 70,000 or more 10-inch rainbow trout. While most of them are caught each summer, a healthy number of them make it to the second, third, and fourth years, and 15- to 18-inch fish are caught regularly. Weighted Woolly Buggers in purple, black, or gold should be bounced along the bottom from a float tube 50 to 100 feet from shore or full strip retrieved by casting toward the shore and retrieved to deeper water. From the bank smaller rainbows can be caught by casting nymphs and emergers out past the weed beds and using the wrist roll (short) retrieves in to shore.

Admission is charged per vehicle, and no gasoline-powered boats are allowed on the lake, although electric motors on rafts and small boats are allowed.

For more information call Aurora Reservoir headquarters at (303) 690-1286.

APPENDIX A
FAMILIAR FLIES BY SEASON

Summer

The Banksia Bug is an excellent caddis emerger that can be fished dead-drifted or swung into the current downstream and then lifted, either by itself or as part of a dry/dropper combination. The Clown Shoe Caddis dry fly is an excellent choice for the top fly.

One of the most effective flies ever invented, the Beadhead Prince Nymph can imitate a stonefly or caddis nymph, or is effective as an attractor. The two largest fish I've ever caught were both on #16 Prince Nymphs, and both came at times when other anglers weren't catching fish.

Beadhead Prince Nymphs in size 6 to 10 are primarily used during large stonefly or salmonfly hatches.

The Kaufmann's or K's Stonefly Nymph, in black, brown or gold, with or without rubber legs, is used when stoneflies are present. These flies are lead wrapped beneath the dubbing so they don't require additional weight.

While Woolly Buggers come in a wide-range of colors, black, brown, gold, and olive are the most effective for trout. Pink and purple can also work for Kokanee. Use bead heads (both cones and beads) for getting deep, but keep them unweighted for low water.

Clown Shoe Caddis flies are excellent during caddis hatches and serve as a good top fly, especially in tandem with caddis larvae, a Banksia Bug, or a Prince Nymph.

One of the most realistic mayfly nymphs going, the Crown Jewel Green Drake works especially well when drakes (green, brown, or gray) are on the water.

A realistic looking nymph, the Golden Stonefly can be fished anytime during the summer months, either singly or as part of a dry/dropper or double nymph rig.

Even when there is no caddis activity present, caddis larvae can be in the water, building their houses, moving around, getting washed loose. Caddis larvae flies are very good by themselves or as the dropper off a dry fly.

When you can see caddis activity on the water, chances are that the pupae are even more active below. They are transitioning into adults, and once they reach that stage, waste no time getting to the surface and flying away. Trout take the larvae very aggressively. Fish this fly across and down, letting it swing into the current, either singly or as the dropper on a dry fly.

The standard emerger for mayflies, the Hare's Ear can also be used to imitate other species as well. The flies come in gray, olive, and tan, and with or without beads. All of them can be effective.

La Fontaine's Sparkle Caddis Emerger should be fished in a fashion similar to the Banksia Bug. It can be equally effective.

ALL FLY PHOTOS BY RON BAIRD

The New Green Stimmie is just a Stimulator with a sleeker body and a few strands of crystal flash tied into the body. It has been such an effective fly for so long, it belongs in various sizes and colors in every angler's fly box. An attractor fly that rides high in the water, it is used as a green drake adult, a hopper, or who knows what. The fish love them. As a hopper in a hopper/dropper rig they are killers, particularly when paired with a smaller beadhead or unweighted Prince Nymph.

An Orange Stimulator works well when there are salmonflies on the water.

A good hopper pattern is invaluable for late summer to early fall. I like the parachute because the sight post keeps it visible in choppy water. The brightly colored foam hoppers are primarily used as strike indicators in a hopper-dropper rig because they stay afloat and will hold weighted flies up in the water column.

There are too many effective PMD dry flies to recommend any one in particular, but I like this one because of its flash sight post for easy watching.

The Royal Wulff is the classic dry fly and may be responsible for bringing more fish to hand than any other.

Blue-winged olives are more prominent in the spring and fall but can be found in the summer. This "spent" BWO represents the insect as it's dead or dying, at the end of its life cycle. Many anglers believe these patterns are more effective than dry flies imitating live insects.

Fall/Winter/Spring

Apart from a few summer flies that carry over, the main aquatic insects of the fall are blue-winged olive mayflies (or baetis), of which there are dozens of sizes and shades, and midges, of which there are hundreds of sizes and shades. In the coldest months of winter, there are only midges, and in the spring, BWOs and midges.

The brassie is simply a tiny hook, wrapped in fine copper thread with a clump of thread or peacock herl just below the eyelet to imitate a midge larval form.

A higher tech version of the San Juan worm made famous on the San Juan River below Navajo Dam in New Mexico, the I.E.D. works best in higher than average water. If the conditions are right, when fished in combination with an egg pattern, it will work unbelievably well.

The Juju Baetis pattern imitates one of the intermediate sizes of a baetis emerger.

This Jujubee Midge pattern represents an intermediate size of a midge emerger.

Representing a blue-winged olive emerger, the clear bead on the Mercury BWO gives it its Mercury designation.

The Parawulff BWO is a standard hackle BWO adult in sizes #16 to #24 but with two white wings to be used as sight posts.

Egg imitations should be dead-drifted in sizes #12 to #18 in the spring. At the right times, they're a sure bet.

The Rainbow Mickey Finn is a top- to mid-water streamer that imitates a rainbow trout fry.

The Rainbow Zonker should sometimes be fished with added weight to get it down to streambed.

The Rojo Midge Emerger represents a tiny, bloodworm emerger.

Small, black stoneflies appear in all running water in the fall, winter, and spring, and will always take fish. Look for patterns in sizes #10 to #16.

An all-around fly, the RS-2 comes in a variety of colors, and can represent the emerging forms of both midges and blue-winged olives, depending upon the color. Not a few anglers have said if they could use only one fly, it would be an RS-2.

With its bead head, the Thin Mint bead submerges relatively fast, but works better in shallow to intermediate depths.

Except for the bead, the Zebra Midge looks like the larval form of the average midge.

APPENDIX B
WADING SAFETY

The most important advice I ever received about wading was to be sure that the water downstream was safe. If you slip and fall into the water, are you going to be able to get out downstream? If the water below you is faster than where you're currently wading, you are better off finding another, safer spot.

Also avoid water that would make landing a big fish difficult.

Equipment will not necessarily keep you from falling in, but it might keep you from being swept downstream. A wading staff and good, rubber- or felt-soled boots will help keep you upright. But waders with no belt might turn into an upside-down water parachute if you fall, adding 10 to 15 pounds of water to each leg and increasing the speed at which you move downstream. Be leery of spikes on felt or rubber soles. They might make sense on snow or ice, but they'll slide like ice skates over smooth stones. Felt is also a greater risk in terms of potentially transmitting whirling disease and mud snails. The new, soft rubber soles for wading seem to be gaining popularity.

When wading try to keep both legs parallel to the bank. That reduces the drag. If you have to turn around, try to find a buffer, such as a large rock in the stream, to turn. Standing in front of the rock is best. Current will often dig a hole behind a rock. Be sure your lead foot is on a solid stream base before you move the second foot. A wading staff will always give you two points of connection with the stream bottom.

Dragging your rod downstream also helps you keep your balance in fast current. Always be able to see the bottom. Falling in the water need not always be fatal to be bad. It can ruin a fishing trip as fast as anything I know.

APPENDIX C
STREAM FLOW CHARTS

To look at current stream flow conditions, search www.dwr.state.co.us/SurfaceWater/default.aspx, and pick a watershed by clicking on the watersheds in the black bar across the top. Scroll down to the name of the fishery, and look to the right for "value" in the third column. That will give you the current (no pun intended) stream flow. Some of these rivers, for instance the Arkansas, can have dozens of listings. You may have to get out a map to determine exactly what stretch of water this is covering. For example, one listing is "Arkansas River near Leadville." That's pretty much the top of the river. Others say "Arkansas River at Granite" or "Arkansas River at Parkdale."

If you click on the name "Arkansas River at Granite," you will see approximately 10 days of stream flow data up to the current day in the form of a graph. At the bottom of the graph are choices for data: 3 Day, 10 Day, 1 Month, Water Year.

Some of these selections will say beneath the river name in green "Corps of Engineers," or "U.S. Geological Survey." Click on the river name, and in the blue bar a third of the way down the page will be "Real time data." Flows for one week will be displayed in the second graph down. For longer periods scroll down to "Daily data."

Play with this feature, and get used to using it. Many of the fly shops will include daily, even up-to-the-minute, flows. But it takes a bit of searching to find a shop that shows data for the stretch of water you are looking for.

APPENDIX D
New Zealand Mud Snail and Zebra and Quagga Mussel Control

The precautions against mud snail spreading are also the same for whirling disease, a blight that's found pretty much everywhere except in high mountain streams. Zebra and quagga mussels are also a threat to Colorado lakes. Mandatory checkpoints manned by volunteers are set up at almost all major lakes, and boats and other equipment must be certified as mussel free to be allowed on the water.

One way to control the spread of snails (and whirling disease) might be the use of rubber-soled wading boots. The theory is that organisms hitchhike in more porous felt soles. But certain control steps endorsed by the Colorado Division of Wildlife are still necessary. Any wading gear or clothes should be cleaned in the manner described on the CDOW website. While you can clean your gear by submerging it in Formula 409 or industrial cleaner, for my money the more practical methods involve either putting your boots and waders in the freezer overnight or letting them dry out for at least 10 days.

For information on identifying New Zealand mud snails and preventing their spread (and that of other invasive species), see the Colorado Division of Wildlife website: http://wildlife.state.co.us/. The page devoted to mud snails is http://wildlife.state.co.us/WildlifeSpecies/Profiles/InvasiveSpecies/NewZealandMudsnail.htm.

For information on zebra and quagga mussel control in Colorado, see http://wildlife.state.co.us/WildlifeSpecies/Profiles/Invasive\Species/ZebraandQuaggaMussels.htm.

APPENDIX E
Colorado Fly Shops, Outfitters, and Guides

To find out the current fishing conditions, check the fly shop websites for "fishing reports." Some of these are so thorough, so detailed it almost makes it seem too easy. But don't kid yourself. Yes, they are invaluable, but they are not going to guarantee anything. That's why they call it "fishing," not "catching."

*Denotes thorough, detailed, year-round fishing reports

**Denotes, in addition to above, archived fishing reports or other in-depth reference material

Gunnison River in Gunnison Gorge

Black Canyon Anglers
7904 Shea Rd.
PO Box 180
Austin, CO 81410
(970) 835-5050
www.blackcanyonanglers.com*
info@blackcanyonanglers.com

Cimarron Creek
317 E. Main St.
Montrose, CO 81401
(970) 249-0408
www.cimarroncreek.com

RIGS Flyshop
565 Sherman, Suite 2
PO Box 2086
Ridgway, CO 81432
(970) 626-4460
www.fishrigs.com
info@fishrigs.com

Gunnison River Expeditions
4770 Scenic Mesa Rd.
Hotchkiss, CO 81419
(970) 874-8184
www.gunnisonriverexpeditions.com
E-mail through website

Taylor River

Dragonfly Anglers
307 Elk Ave.
Crested Butte, CO 81224
(800) 491-3079
www.dragonflyanglers.com*
info@dragonflyanglers.com

Willowfly Anglers
130 CR 742
PO Box 339
Almont, CO 81210
(888) 761-FISH
www.willowflyanglers.com*
fish@willowflyanglers.com

Gunnison River Fly Shop
300 North Main St.
Gunnison, CO 81230
(970) 641-2930
www.gunnisonriverflyshop.com
info@gunnisonriverflyshop.com

**Fryingpan River,
Roaring Fork River**
Taylor Creek Fly Shops
183 Basalt Center Circle
PO Box 799
Basalt, CO 81621
(970) 927-4374
408 East Cooper Street
Aspen, CO 81611
(970) 920-1128
www.taylorcreek.com**
tcreek@ssv.net

Roaring Fork Anglers
Roaring Fork Anglers
2205 Grand Ave.
Glenwood Springs, CO 81601
(970) 945-0180
www.roaringforkanglers.com**
info@roaringforkanglers

Alpine Angling
995 Cowen Dr., Suite 102
Carbondale, CO 81623
(970) 963-9245
www.roaringforkanglers.com*
info@roaringforkanglers

Fryingpan Anglers
132 Basalt Center Circle
PO Box 4524
Basalt, CO 81621
(970) 927-3441
www.fryingpananglers.com**
report@fryingpananglers.com

Lake Fork of the Gunnison River
Gunnison River Fly Shop
300 North Main St.
Gunnison, CO 81230
(970) 641-2930
www.gunnisonriverflyshop.com
info@gunnisonriverflyshop.com

**The Sportsman Outdoors &
Fly Shop**
238 S. Gunnison
PO Box 340
Lake City, CO 81235
(970) 944-2526
www.lakecitysportsman.com
info@ lakecitysportsman.com

Dan's Fly Shop
723 Gunnison Ave.
PO Box 220
Lake City, CO 81235
(970) 944-2281 (summer)
(970) 252-9106 (winter)
www.dansflyshop.com
dansflyshop@lakecity.net

South Platte River in
Eleven Mile Canyon
Blue Quill Angler
1532 Bergen Pkwy.
Evergreen, CO 80439
(303) 674-4700
www.bluequillangler.com**
flyfish@bluequillangler.com

The Peak Fly Shop
5767 N. Academy Blvd.
Colorado Springs, CO 80918
(719) 260-1415
301 E. Hwy 24
Woodland Park, CO 80863
(719) 687-9122
www.thepeakflyshop.com**
thepeakflyshop@gmail.com

Cache La Poudre River
St. Peter's Fly Shop
202 Remington St.
Ft. Collins, CO 80524
(970) 498-8968
www.stpetes.com*
shop@stpetes.com

Big Thompson River
Front Range Anglers
2344 Pearl St.
Boulder, CO 80302
(303) 494-1375
www.frontrangeanglers.com**
info@frontrangeanglers.com

St. Peter's Fly Shop
202 Remington St.
Ft. Collins, CO 80524
(970) 498-8968
www.stpetes.com**
shop@stpetes.com

Estes Angler
338 W. Riverside Dr.
PO Box 1703
Estes Park, CO 80517
(970) 586-2110
(800) 586-2110
www.estesangler.com
info@estesangler.com

Kirk's Fly Shop
230 E. Elkhorn Ave.
Estes Park, CO 80517
(970) 577-0790
(877) 669-1859
www.kirksflyshop.com
E-mail through the website

Trappers Lake
Wyatt's Sports Center
223 8th St.
Meeker, CO 81641
(970) 878-4428

Blue River, Williams Fork River below Williams Fork Reservoir

Cutthroat Anglers
400 Blue River Parkway
Silverthorne, CO 80498
(970) 262-2878
www.fishcolorado.com**
anglers@fishcolorado.com

Blue Quill Angler
1532 Bergen Pkwy.
Evergreen, CO 80439
(303) 674-4700
www.bluequillangler.com**
flyfish@bluequillangler.com

Blue River Anglers
281 Main St.
Frisco, CO 80443
(888) 453-9171
www.blueriveranglers.com
info@blueriveranglers.com

Breckenridge Outfitters
101 North Main St., Suite B
PO Box 6237
Breckenridge, CO 80424
(970) 453-4135
www.breckenridgeoutfitters.com
info@breckenridgeoutfitters.com

Bull Basin Guides and Outfitters
Dean Billington, Owner
PO Box 1566
Kremmling, CO 80459
office (970) 724-0417
cell (970) 485-3236
fax (970) 724-0292
www.bullbasin.com
www.troublesomeflyfishing.com
info@bullbasin.com

Arkansas River

Royal Gorge Anglers
1210 Royal Gorge Blvd.
Cañon City, CO 81212
(719) 269-3474
(888) 994-6743
www.royalgorgeanglers.com**
bill@royalgorgeanglers.com

Arkansas River Fly Shop
7500 W. Hwy. 50
Salida, CO 81201
(719) 539-4223
www.arkanglers.com
info@arkanglers.com

ArkAnglers
517 US Hwy. 24 S.
Buena Vista, CO 81211
(719) 395-1796
www.arkanglers.com
info@arkanglers.com

INDEX

ABOUT THE AUTHOR

Ron Baird is a retired award-winning journalist. He is the author of *Dark Angel,* a mystery described as "A Tale of Murder, Mayhem and Flyfishing," and a new sequel, *Black Wind.* He's also written *Fishing Colorado,* a FalconGuide. He and his wife, Nancy Morrell, live in the foothills of Boulder, Colorado.

PHOTO BY NANCY MORRELL